Regulating Emotion the DBT Way

Regulating Emotion the DBT Way is a practical guide to the DBT skill of 'Opposite Action', which helps clients develop the skill of up- or down-regulating their emotions when necessary. It is the skill that fosters emotional literacy in clients who have learned to fear or avoid painful feelings.

Part A of the text introduces emotion theory, describes how to validate emotions, and explains how Linehan's 'Opposite Action' skill is used to regulate problematic responses. There are examples and analogies that can be shared with clients, and clinical examples to demonstrate the key points. There is a description of how DBT therapists contextualise emotion using chain analysis. Part B dedicates a chapter to each of the basic emotions and describes its signature features. A session scenario is included allowing the reader to see how the therapist coaches the skill of opposite action, elicits behavioural rehearsal, and gives corrective feedback. There are some tips on handling common issues specific to that emotion, based on the author's extensive experience.

This book will be of interest to any therapist who wants to learn more about a behavioural approach to emotion such as psychologists, nurses, social workers, psychiatrists, counsellors, cognitive therapists, prison staff, and occupational therapists. It is an accessible explanation of emotion regulation for people who have already undertaken DBT training.

Christine Dunkley, DClinP, is a consultant trainer with the British Isles DBT training team, and a fellow of the Society for DBT in the UK and Ireland. She has 20 years of working experience with self-harming patients in the NHS.

Regulating Emotion the DBT Way

A Therapist's Guide to Opposite Action

Christine Dunkley

Routledge
Taylor & Francis Group

LONDON AND NEW YORK

First published 2021
by Routledge
2 Park Square, Milton Park, Abingdon, Oxon OX14 4RN

and by Routledge
52 Vanderbilt Avenue, New York, NY 10017

Routledge is an imprint of the Taylor & Francis Group, an informa business

© 2021 Christine Dunkley

British Library Cataloguing-in-Publication Data
A catalogue record for this book is available from the British Library

Library of Congress Cataloging-in-Publication Data
A catalog record has been requested for this book

ISBN: 978-0-367-25920-4 (hbk)
ISBN: 978-0-367-25921-1 (pbk)
ISBN: 978-0-429-29053-4 (ebk)

Typeset in Optima
by codeMantra

To John Dunkley, Laura Dunkley, Lucy Darby,
Matt Darby and Silver Kate Darby

Contents

Contents

Acknowledgements

Deep gratitude to the clients with whom I have worked over the years, who taught me so much. Also to Marsha Linehan for her inspirational career and therapeutic genius.

Thank you to my beloved gurus Michaela Swales and Heidi Heard for their clinical excellence, and for setting by example their standard for the British Isles DBT (BI-DBT) Training team. Special gratitude to Amy Gaglia who is my personal sounding board, longstanding friend and stalwart confidante, who helped clarify a number of complex points. Appreciation to Janet Feigenbaum, my DBT twin in our trainer careers. Thank you also to Becky Wallace for helping get this book into print. and to all my colleagues at BI-DBT: Richard, Carolyn, Jim, Maggie, Stephanie, Dan, Ceri, Brandon, Roo, Barbara, Angie, and Michelle.

Acknowledgements to my co-volunteers in the Society for DBT, especially my best friends Pamela Henderson and Emily Fox, who along with Amy make all our DBT adventures enjoyable. To Stephen Palmer, thank you for your consistent encouragement and sage advice. To all those who uphold the work at the Linehan Institute, thank you for your regular welcome at the trainers meeting. Personal thanks for exceptional kindness to Jennifer Sayrs, Tony Du Bose, and Sara Schmidt.

Introduction

I came to dialectical behaviour therapy (DBT) by a meandering route. In 1984 I was a young medical social worker in an Accident and Emergency department, where I would be called to see any patient who had taken an overdose the night before. My instruction was 'get this person out of hospital and keep them out for 30 days' because a readmission within a month was classed as a faulty discharge. I think I was as traumatised as the patients as I accompanied them to evacuate terrible accommodation, tackle volatile partners, return to empty homes after bereavements, attend court, flee to refuges, cope with permanent disability, tend sick dependents, or manage on impossibly low incomes. Bonding with people at the peak of their crises I was deeply affected by their stories; repeated descriptions of intense and intolerable emotional pain. It was clear that sexual abuse histories were a recurring theme, so I undertook further counselling training to help clients work through those issues. Unfortunately this did not go as planned, I soon realised that people who were already suicidal either could not tolerate the emotions raised by counselling or had revisited their story many times but still felt tortured.

In 1994 I was hired in a psychology department seeing patients for counselling and it was there that I heard about DBT, the missing link that would help people manage their emotions before addressing the underlying trauma. Marsha Linehan (although she had not at that time revealed her personal trauma history) described perfectly the obstacles I had observed in my own clinical work, and offered some insightful and novel solutions. I had found my spiritual home! A group of us trained and set up the Winchester DBT programme in 2001.

To me, the programmatic element of DBT was one of its selling points. Linehan understood that for people who want to die, the level of intervention has to match the level of their pain. A DBT programme is a fairly hefty intervention:

1) A community of therapists treats each client. This consultation team meets weekly, ensuring there is always more than one perspective, and minimising 'drift' from the model.

2) The client attends a weekly skills class which Linehan likens to learning to put up your tent in back garden before having to erect it on the side of a mountain in a hurricane. The group is run more like a French grammar class, learning the skill and how to use it, having a practice and getting feedback.

3) An individual therapist meets weekly with the client to re-run the most problematic moment of the week, substituting more skilful behaviour. The client learns how to implement skills in their unique circumstances.

4) Clients are also given out-of hours-telephone contact, so that they can get in vivo coaching from their therapist during evenings and weekends. (Don't panic – this is done within the therapist's limits.)

5) Carers, allied professionals, families, and other helpers have opportunities to receive information (perhaps through groups or consultation). The aim is to structure environments to facilitate more skills use.

I have to admit that when I heard about the out-of-hours telephone contact I assumed immediately that it would be a nightmare to deliver, and that I would feel as though I was never away from work. In reality this was my favourite part of the therapy. It was through doing these coaching calls that I got to find out what actually works. Not what 'works in theory' or 'could work if they did it right' or 'might have worked if X or Y hadn't happened'. In those coal-face conversations it was my clients who taught me most about regulating emotion, about what helps, and what can go wrong. We taught each other to have confidence in the skills, and we concluded that Linehan really knew her stuff.

I also had lots of guidance from my supervisor Dr Heidi Heard, who had done the original trials with Linehan, and from our own international DBT guru Professor Michaela Swales, Director of the British Isles Training team, which I joined in 2006. These two women tutored me regularly, patiently, and with clinical brilliance, for which I am eternally grateful.

As I did more DBT training, listening to supervision tapes and consulting to teams, I realised that too often therapists were coaching distress tolerance. Although clients were being taught emotion regulation skills in group, these were not being strengthened by behavioural rehearsal during one-to-one sessions. The clients were learning to tolerate emotional distress rather than becoming more emotionally literate. I learnt with the help of supervisees and training delegates to nudge therapists more towards emotion regulation, and contributed a chapter on this topic to The Oxford Handbook of Dialectical Behaviour Therapy, which was well received (Dunkley, 2018) In 2019 I presented an exemplar lecture for the worldwide DBT trainers meeting on this topic. I received confirmation from my peers that this was not just a UK issue.

And so I wrote this book to give practical advice for therapists who want to improve their coaching of emotion regulation with clients during individual therapy. My particular focus is just one amazing skill called Opposite Action, the DBT version of teaching emotional literacy. In my view it captures the very essence of dialectics because the client must learn discernment, not just between emotions, but in their strength and function. They learn to assess how much emotion is justified in a given moment, and how to either up- or down-regulate their response to match the facts.

Emotion regulation is not a 'quick' intervention, and nor is it simple, which perhaps explains why some therapists lean more towards distraction. However, if coached skilfully it drastically changes the client's relationship with their internal environment. It adds something so deliciously, unexpectedly *valuable*, that clients begin to welcome rather than fear their emotional experiences.

I hope it does not come as a disappointment that I am not outlining the whole raft of skills in the emotion regulation module – that has already been done in Linehan's skill's training manual (2015a, 2015b) and accompanying worksheets, and I cannot improve upon them. These books are the go-to resource for DBT therapy, and if you have not yet read them I encourage you to do so. But I also hope to foster in this small niche the love for dialectics and opposite action that I have myself, having seen at firsthand how it can transform the lives of clients who had often given up hope.

I illustrate the text with anecdotes and scenarios that are based in real clinical encounters. These have been trimmed or embellished to disguise the identity of the client. Sometimes material from two or three clinical cases will be combined to demonstrate a point. So although the clients in the book are not real people their material is based in fact.

When I say 'you' in the text I am referring to you the therapist, unless otherwise specified. When I say 'we' I am sometimes just including myself in this group, and at others referring to 'we humans', I hope that the distinction will be clear. I vary the gender pronouns because these things apply to people generically. If I over-use female references it is because as an outpatient community therapist I saw mostly women of child-rearing age, so I have more clinical examples from that group. However in the last decade I've consulted widely in settings from prisons to children's homes, as the population receiving DBT has grown. I also have experience of DBT implementation in other cultures, though the majority of my clinical work has been in the UK NHS and Irish HSE.

The book is in two parts: First the theory of emotion regulation, and then practical issues relating to each emotion, including a segment of therapy demonstrating how the therapist drilled home the steps in emotion regulation experientially, through encouraging the client to rehearse in session. Each emotion has cropped up during a chain and solution analysis, and in each case the therapist moves in to teach the client how to regulate their emotion in that specific context. Finally there is a summary chapter with some trouble-shooting. You may start reading from the beginning, or if you are already familiar with the early material just dip into the emotion-specific chapters as and when they become relevant to your client work.

References

Dunkley, C. (2018) Conceptual and practical issues in the application of emotion regulation in dialectical behaviour therapy. In Swales, M. A. (Ed.), *The Oxford handbook of dialectical behaviour therapy*. Oxford: Oxford University Press.

Linehan, M. (2015a). *DBT skills training manual*, 2nd ed.. Guilford Publications.

Linehan, M. (2015b). *DBT skills training handouts and worksheets*, 2nd ed.. Guilford Publications.

PART A

Emotion regulation theory

This section of the book covers the general theory of emotions as they are conceptualised in DBT.

The chapters cover a definition of emotions, their functions, and forms; how to provide emotion validation; and the importance of problem-solving as an emotion regulation skill.

This information sets the scene for the emotion-specific chapters that follow in Part B

Emotion regulation and dialectics

What is emotion regulation?

Imagine the following scenario:

> You are working as a therapist for a large organisation, and
> for the last three months your salary has been paid below
> the amount you are due. Each time you have called the pay-
> roll section and given them all the information they need to
> pay you correctly, and have received numerous assurances
> that it would not happen again. Now payday comes around
> and you eagerly scan your payslip. Once again there is an
> error, this time you are underpaid by an even larger amount
> than last month. Instantly you feel angry, but the first cli-
> ent of the day is due to arrive. You take a deep breath and
> put a smile on your face, dropping your shoulders down as
> you greet them. You soon forget your pay problem, as you
> are engrossed in the session, but at lunchtime you call pay-
> roll. Unfortunately this time the administrator you speak to
> is new, and knows little of your backstory. Despite feeling
> very annoyed you recognise that this person is not to blame,
> so you tone down your anger somewhat. You still keep
> your voice firm as you request a call back at the earliest

opportunity from their colleague. You are told it will probably be tomorrow. That evening you recount the story to your
spouse and give vent to the full annoyance you feel. Your
partner shares your frustration and in response to their validating replies your anger subsides. Not completely, though,
as the matter cannot be finally resolved until you speak to
payroll again the next day.

What you have done on this occasion is a perfect example of
emotion regulation. First, you had an appropriately angry response to the trigger of the incorrect payment. Next you ad-
justed for a situation where this anger would be unhelpful by
using some physiological strategies and refocussing your attention on your client. But you did not *forget* the anger, you used it
as motivation to problem-solve the payment issue. Despite being ready to let rip on the phone to the payroll clerk, you used
some perspective-taking and correctly assessed that this was
unjustified, as she was new and trying to help. So you dialled
the anger down to fit the circumstances, but not all the way
to zero because the irritation in your voice-tone was necessary
to communicate urgency. When you were with your partner
you expressed your anger more fully, which elicited validation.
You retained just enough annoyance to keep the matter 'live'
for you, resolving to return to problem-solving the next day.

During this process you did not simply *supress* your anger, by which I would mean 'struggle to hide it whilst feeling
like you were about to burst'. Instead you employed different
devices – mindfulness, physical strategies, discernment, and
problem-solving – in the correct combination to get the best
outcome. Sometimes you dampened the anger down, at others
you increased the intensity of it.

A common misconception about emotion is that to be regulated it has to be lowered or eradicated. If that were the case,
then the skill would be called 'Emotion Reduction', or even

'Emotion Elimination'. An emotion may be high and still justified by the facts. For example, during a recent fire in a university hall of residence students started shouting and banging on doors to rouse their friends. This level of emotion was completely appropriate to the situation.

Emotion regulation as taught in DBT is a complex set of skills designed to help clients who find their emotions painfully intense, who are emotion-phobic, or who numb out from their feelings. To learn emotional literacy is hard for people who experience emotion as uncomfortable waves of sensation, pulsing through their body and clouding their reason. It's a brave step to trust that these uninvited internal phenomena can be useful in everyday life. At the other end of the scale there are people for whom intense emotions are not the problem, but rather society's inability to accommodate their responses. It's our aim to champion emotions as the instruments in an orchestra, from triangle to big bass drum. We don't call the tune, or set the taste of the audience, we help if there is discordance.

Therapists naturally want to avoid subjecting clients to distress, particularly if this can drive them to harmful activities. After all, DBT is best known as a treatment for people with extreme levels of emotional pain, those who have been hospitalised for multiple suicide attempts or dangerous self-harming. Perhaps they are in prison for attacking others, or are being treated for addictions. Linehan's theory is that for these people their emotions rise up more quickly than average, peak at an unusually high intensity, and have a slower return to baseline. It is during this cycle of physical discomfort that the client seeks relief, often believing that an emotion will never reduce unless they actively *do something* to make it stop.

Almost all behaviours that bring clients to mental health services either function to reduce an unpleasant emotion or happen as a result of one. Let's take suicidality as an example. Ligaturing creates a dissociative light-headedness that carries with it the promise of eventual oblivion. Overdosing can have the same effect. Just *thinking* about being dead offers the enticing prospect of freedom from emotional torture. It is common for people to state after a suicide attempt, 'I just wanted to be out of it'. Linehan sums this up in the phrase, 'suicide is their solution'.

Other behaviours also offer emotional relief. Drinking and drug-taking have obvious anaesthetising effects. Severe social withdrawal limits access to emotional cues (binge-watching Netflix behind closed doors is preferable to braving those unpredictable triggers in the outside world.) Impulsive behaviours such as shoplifting, aggressive outbursts, binge-eating, or reckless driving can satisfy an intense emotional urge. Sometimes the client has acted without conscious decision; *'My partner makes me so angry it's like a red mist coming down and I just lash out, I can't help it'.*

Finally, self-harming behaviours such as cutting and burning can change the way the emotion is experienced in the body. The physical pain of self-harm may distract the person from their emotional torment. Or if the client is numb before they cut themselves, the feeling can restore a sense of reality. When people fear their mental pain will never subside, substituting a physical wound might serve to reassure them that it will fade as the tissue-damage heals.

It's not an easy task to explain to clients that their emotions could be of interest, rather than just horrible sensations. I sometimes tell them the story of when I was about 22, back in the early eighties. My friend bought a rusty old banger from a guy in a pub. Needless to say he got what he paid for; a car that was only just roadworthy. He told me that he was worried about a warning light that kept flashing on the dashboard, as he had no idea what it meant. This was pre-internet, so he couldn't just look it up (apologies to those of you who have just been traumatised by the idea of no internet.) A few days later I saw him again and enquired about the light. He told me cheerfully that he had sorted it out.

'Ah, good news, so what was it for?' I asked.

'I don't know,' he replied. 'I managed to prise the dash-board open with my screwdriver just enough to get my clip-pers behind, so that I could snip the wire...'

We all recognise that this was a bad idea. Yet it is the perfect metaphor for the actions of clients who suffer intense painful emotions. They no longer want to understand what the feeling is trying to tell them, they just want to snip the wire. For these clients we have some bad news and some good news.

The bad news is that emotion regulation is time-consuming and complicated to learn. It will involve staying with some un-pleasant bodily experiences slightly longer than they really want, and trying to decipher what each one signifies. It will mean ac-tively keeping around some unpleasant sensations like anger or sadness sometimes because, well, that's what is needed in the moment.

The good news is that at the end of the DBT programme it is possible that each new emotion coming into their body will be a welcome guest, bringing with it a valuable source of infor-mation, acting as a useful guide. They can have confidence that if an emotion is too intense they can reduce it without resorting to drastic means. They will no longer feel as though an emotion just settles in for the week. They will be able to increase some emotions when they are necessary, and then let them go when they have served their usefulness. In short, Linehan says they can learn to love their emotions.

Taking a dialectical approach

The skill of Opposite Action is a method of working out what level of emotion is justified by a given situation, and then either increasing the amount that is needed, or decreasing it, according to how much emotion fits the facts. There are other skills in the emotion regulation module in DBT, but this particular one is what I think of as the jewel in the crown, because it is the most dialectical of them all. But what do we mean by 'dialectical?' For anyone not familiar with dialectics a pithy definition is, 'It depends'. A dialectical stance is the exact opposite of black-and-white thinking.

We already know that a rigid or extreme approach, and the inability to see other perspectives, is associated with poor mental health (Morris and Mansell 2018). Flexibility and openness to a wide range of views enable us to maximise our resources and coping strategies. Dialectics encapsulates that ability to move fluidly to another solution if the one we are using is not working, or to switch perspectives. An example of a dialectical approach is 'if you pull on the door-handle and the door doesn't open, try pushing'. Or 'If you look left and there is no way out, look right, in fact look up and down too'. The ability to adapt to incremental changes in a situation is another dialectical skill, unlike the toad that if placed in a pan of cool water will simply sit there till it boils. Dialectics would say – while the water is cool stay in, and when it gets hot, jump out. Adopting a dialectical philosophy means being willing to swerve, reverse, advance, hold firm, settle, sink, or soar as needed. There is no 'one-size-fits-all'.

Dialectics goes further than suggesting we just widen our viewpoint. It espouses the idea that whilst two views might appear to be polar opposites, it is possible for them to co-exist. For example, consider these statements; 'I love my job' and 'I hate my job'. I am sure that most of us have wavered between these two positions about the same job, maybe even flowing back and forth in the same day. It's not as if when you love your job all the reasons for hating it go away, or when you hate it, there is nothing to like at all. It's complicated. The position you take in any given moment is likely to be influenced by the context – whether a client just told you that your intervention saved their life, or whether you're expected to do eight tasks with only the time and resources to do three. So nothing stays the same, and everything is subjected to influence.

As DBT therapists, we might say that we are 'influence analysers'. Rather than reject one position as bad and the other as good, we establish which factors strengthen either end of that polarity. We are interested in how we stack the deck to make, in this case, 'liking your job' come out on top, and 'hating your job' recede to the bottom. A dialectician is looking for controlling variables, to see how to tweak them to get the best out of any situation.

If we look at the dialectic of loving your job. Perhaps you have a better day at work if the person you share your office with appears cheerful. She, in turn, finds her mood is lifted if her partner is happy. Let's say he is a green-grocer and supplies local restaurants with fresh produce. He gets stressed if he cannot meet his orders. Your satisfaction at work may now depend on the availability of avocados. So another law of dialectics is that everything is in relationship, everything is connected. Turn one cog, and a number of them also turn, ad infinitum. Nothing stays the same, everything happens in a swirling net of interconnected systems.

Once we understand this we can see the futility of saying, *'if you get angry do X or do Y'.* It depends on the trigger for the anger, the situation in which it occurs, the intensity of it, the duration of it, and how it might function to help you. Each emotion can only be seen as regulated or dysregulated by exploring the context.

We are always trying to establish whether the emotional intensity is appropriate using the skill called, 'Check the Facts' (Linehan 2015b pg 285). It is important to state here that the CBT skill of the same name is about collecting evidence for or against a cognition. Linehan's skill might be better named, 'Match the Facts' because of its focus on regulating an emotional response to the facts of the situation.

The following teaching scenario can be used to teach this concept to your clients:

Draw a column on the flipchart, representing a scale showing 100% at the top, and zero at the bottom.

Let's say the emotion is guilt.

100% is the *most* guilt you could possibly feel and 0% is no guilt at all.

1) How much guilt would fit the facts if you were meeting a friend for coffee and were ten minutes late because you were stuck in a traffic jam?

2) What if you were an hour late, not because of traffic, but because you decided to stay home a bit longer to watch the end of a TV programme. More guilt or less guilt?

3) What if you didn't turn up at all because you bumped into some other friends on the way and they were just great company (oh, and you were having such a good time you forgot to call ahead and cancel, you just left your friend waiting)?

4) What if you didn't turn up at all because inviting your friend to the coffee shop was a ruse so you could go around and burgle her house? (In this example you might need to up-regulate that guilt. More about that later.)

It is not unusual for the client to say that if they feel guilty about anything at all, it will shoot straight up to 100%. Then I might ask, 'Ok, if being late for coffee is 100%, what if you'd run over her dog in your car?' The most common answer is, 'Then I would feel 200%'. Which of course is against the rules! If you use up all your guilt for a late coffee date, you have nothing in reserve for things that are even worse. If you only have one level of guilt for everything it becomes meaningless. So when we regulate an emotion, we are not trying to get it down to zero, we are trying to get it up or down to roughly the right amount in this moment. Which is why DBT is a mindfulness-based therapy.

The effect we are looking for at this stage is that when a client notices an emotion they stop and think, *hang on a minute, how much of this emotion am I feeling, and how much might fit the facts?* This act of pausing to assess the intensity of feeling is an early step in emotion regulation. Others will be added in later chapters.

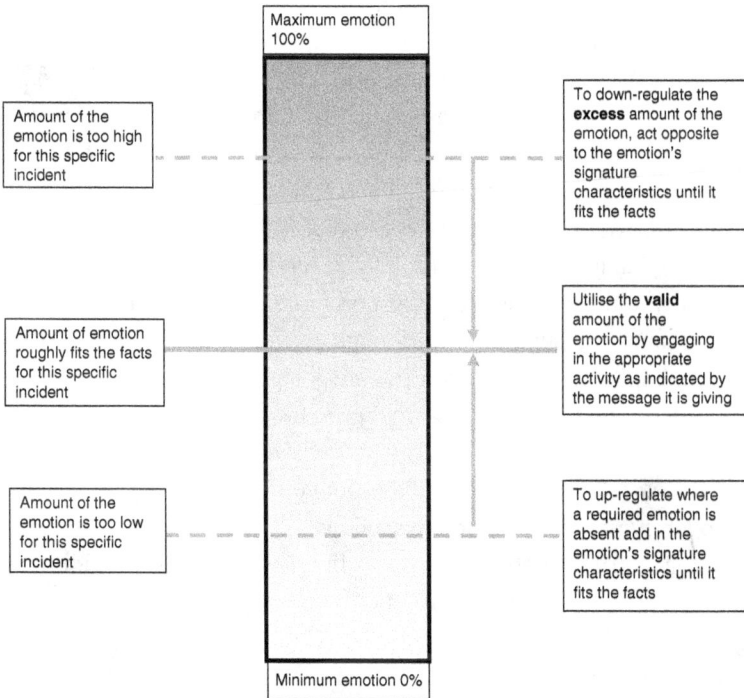

Maximum emotion
100%

Amount of the
emotion is too high
for this specific
incident

To down-regulate the
excess amount of the
emotion, act opposite
to the emotion's
signature
characteristics until it
fits the facts

Amount of emotion
roughly fits the facts
for this specific
incident

Utilise the **valid**
amount of the
emotion by engaging
in the appropriate
activity as indicated by
the message it is giving

Amount of the
emotion is too low
for this specific
incident

To up-regulate where
a required emotion is
absent add in the
emotion's signature
characteristics until it
fits the facts

Minimum emotion 0%

Figure 1.1 Up- or down-regulating emotions to a level that fits the facts.

Solutions also have to be dialectical

Problem-solving is an emotion-regulation strategy. If an emotion is telling you that something is wrong, the most effective thing you can do, above all others, is to fix whatever it is. Then the feeling will have served its purpose and will diminish. More about this in Chapter 5. We use problem-solving for the bit of the emotion that does fit the facts.

In the example above if you were late to the coffee date, then you need to do something to problem-solve justified guilt, because it was trying to tell you something; that your friend suffered some inconvenience and you need to make amends. If you were only ten minutes late it might be enough to acknowledge the transgression, explain about the traffic and apologise. The whole incident could be appeased and forgotten in a few moments. But if you were an hour late without real cause that same brief apology would fall short. Because the offence was greater, your repair would have to match it. You'd probably end up paying for the coffee and maybe sending a card afterwards. You would have to look and sound more contrite, and not rush to change the subject, even though you desperately want to. If you didn't turn up at all then you are going to have to work much harder to repair, perhaps arranging a new outing and turning up early. With flowers. You are going to have to show that you can put *yourself* out as much as you put your friend out. There is a rough symmetry to these transactions.

If you had been involved in burgling your friend's house it's unlikely you'd care that much about repairing the relationship. But if apprehended you might find yourself in some kind of restorative justice programme, paying back not just to the victim but society as a whole. This is a case when emotion needs up-regulating rather than reducing. In the UK we might delay parole for someone who is not showing enough remorse for their crimes. Another example of under-emoting is, say, in a perinatal mental health unit if a mother ignores her crying infant. Such flat affect may be due to post-natal depression, trauma, or burn-out, but such lack of response is a red-flag that means more help is needed before discharge.

Just as the justified amount of the emotion will fluctuate, so too will the solution required to respond appropriately. Even in these examples you can identify some dialectics – factors that will influence the level upwards or downwards. Being ten minutes late because of traffic seems a minor transgression, but what if it was the twelfth time in a row that you were late to meet the same friend? And not turning up at all might be forgiven if your friend was equally flaky. So before jumping to conclusions we would remind ourselves of the DBT mantra – 'Assess don't assume'.

Unfortunately emotions can come so close together that it is hard to discern one from another, or even to notice that the emotions start and stop. Clients say, 'I'm always angry', or 'I feel shame all day every day'. Because they have such aversive experience of emotion, they are often unable to identify which emotion they are feeling, let alone how much of it matches the facts. They lack a vocabulary for their internal phenomena, which is why we emphasise describing the emotion mindfully. Linehan's excellent skills training manual has handouts to help clients distinguish between emotions (Linehan 2015b pgs 214–223) and we will cover more of the emotion signatures in Part B of this book.

Giving information about emotions and their functions can be done in a group or one-to-one. But teaching clients the anatomy of regulation is only half the battle. Strengthening these skills relies on the individual therapist picking out examples and coaching the client through the steps of discerning, raising, or lowering their affect to the required level. The remainder of this book provides a set of examples and guidelines to enhance this process, with lots of clinical examples. I hope it brings to life what you have heard and read elsewhere in your DBT journey, or if you are new to the therapy, that it inspires you to learn more.

References

Linehan, M. (2015b). *DBT skills training handouts and worksheets*, 2nd ed. New York, London: Guilford Publications.

Morris, L., & Mansell, W. (2018). A systematic review of the relationship between rigidity/flexibility and transdiagnostic cognitive and behavioral processes that maintain psychopathology. *Journal of Experimental Psychopathology, 9*(3), 2043808718779431.

CHAPTER 2

Emotion functions and forms

Functions of emotions

Identifying emotions is the first step in regulation, so psycho-education features heavily in the skills training component of DBT. At this point it is advisable to avoid the word 'feeling' because of its additional meanings in every day conversation for varied behavioural phenomena:

- A sensation, e.g. 'last night I got an awful feeling of pins and needles in my big toe'.
- A thought, e.g. 'I just feel like I am being taken for granted'.
- An emotion, e.g. 'I feel really sad'.

Interestingly, under fMRI scanning, 'affect labelling' has been shown to change our neural responses (Torre and Lieberman 2018). This means that even just *naming* an emotion is effective in reducing its intensity. Saying 'I am angry' or 'I am sad' lets the emotion know we are paying attention to it. Whilst it will not completely go away, it will begin to subside a little at that point. Why might this be? In Somatic Marker Theory, Damasio (1996) suggests that complex emotion systems help us prioritise.

We remember the things that create the most powerful body sensations. Once we have acknowledged the emotion by name, then perhaps the brain assumes the marker has hit home and such intensity is no longer required. The naming process utilises the cortex area of the brain which has a dampening effect on the fiery amygdala, the seat of our anxious responses.

Rather than bombard the client with a huge range of options Linehan has wisely chosen a few of the basic emotions. We like to think of these as emotion 'families', so that in the Anger family we would find 'crossness', 'annoyance', 'irritation', and 'frustration'. Every emotion serves a different function and will 'elicit motion' (E-MOTION) by prompting us with an action urge. Below is a brief introduction to each emotion's basic function, and these will be expanded upon in the emotion-specific chapters in Part B.

Anger fits the facts when we are blocked in pursuit of a goal, or when we are threatened. Linehan includes in this category 'when we are in a lot of pain' which might be conceptualised as a type of physical threat. The function of anger is to supply us with a burst of energy, by which we can crash through the obstacle or fend off an aggressor. The action urge of anger is to attack.

Sadness fits the fact when we have suffered a loss. The first function of sadness is to stop us from losing any more, so the initial action urge is to withdraw, which would serve the function of conserving our resources. The second function, which usually comes a little later, is to recover or replace what has been lost, so the action urge associated with this phase is pining for and seeking out the lost person, place, or item. During this phase we are likely to seek out reminders of the source of our grief. Crying and other signs of sadness serve to draw in support from others to help with the search.

Fear fits the facts when we are in danger. Linehan refers to serious risks to your life, health, or well-being. For example, the loss of your home or your livelihood would constitute danger. The function of fear is to keep you safe from harm. Le Doux and Pine (2016) suggest that anxiety occurs when danger is further off, so that there is still a chance to avoid it, whilst pure fear kicks in when the danger is almost on top of us. The action urge for pure fear is to freeze. This might have been an advantage for predator-threats, leaving us cold, immobile, and holding our breath. These actions could help evade detection, or even mimic death to divert animals who prefer live prey.

Joy fits the facts when something is of benefit to us. The function is to help us to maximise our gains by prompting us to repeat this activity. As with other emotions it is possible to have inappropriate joy, e.g. when you have seen your drug dealer, or if you witness others having a hard time.

Guilt fits the facts when we have offended our social group by transgressing the group rules or norms. The function of guilt is to keep us as part of a social group and so the action urge is to repair the transgression. As social rules are seldom written down we tend to assimilate them, which is why Linehan refers to 'breaking your own rules'. I also add in an external frame of reference – have you violated any group norms? – as sometimes the client's internal frame of reference is compromised by their clinical issues.

Shame also fits the facts when we have violated a group rule, but in this case our offence is so terrible that there is a risk of being expelled. Rather than risk trying to make a repair, Shame prompts us to cover up our crime, with the action urge of hiding. This buys time for the incident to blow over and for us to avoid rejection

Disgust fits the facts when there is a risk of contamination through toxins or noxious substances. It helps us avoid infection or poisoning, and the action urge is to repel or recoil from the offending item. We can also feel disgust if there is a risk of social contamination, which is why most people do not want to make friends with paedophiles or racists unless they assume an affiliation with that group.

Envy fits the facts when someone else has something that we would like for ourselves. The function is to get rid of the discrepancy between us, and the action urge is either to attain the coveted item or to destroy it, so that we are no longer unequal.

Jealousy fits the facts when we have something precious and we fear someone else might take it from us. This functions to help us keep our advantages and resources, and the action urge is to jealously guard and protect the things we value highly. On a technical note it is hard to distinguish jealousy and anxiety – the client often describes anxiety sensations, and the behaviours function to try and avoid loss of status.

Therapists need to be very clear on the different emotions, their names, functions, and action urges. Each emotion will be regulated using a different set of strategies, so it is impossible to coach emotion regulation adequately without knowing which one is being regulated. In a dialectical approach, there is no 'one-size-fits-all'.

Emotion signatures

Each emotion plays out in a unique set of physiological and behavioural characteristics. Taken together these domains create a signature look and sound by which the emotion can be identified. At this point I will simply describe the domains, with a few examples. In the second part of this book I will give more detail for each of the basic emotions. Many signatures are immortalised in commonly used phrases, some of which I have included below:

1) **Temperature:** Some emotions are hot, like anger (hot-headed, hot under the collar) and shame (burning with shame). By contrast fear is cold (my blood ran cold).

2) **Facial expression:** Almost every emotion has a signature facial expression. Disgust, e.g. has a distinctive lip curl. (He sneered in disgust.) In fear we become wide-eyed (you could see the whites of their eyes). Anger has a tight mouth (he clenched his jaw, she pursed her lips) and a furrowed brow.

3) **Breathing:** Anger is characterised by a jagged, shortened out-breath (snorting with rage) Sadness has the opposite breath characteristics (he gave a long sigh).

4) **Muscle tone:** Fear has very tense muscles whereas in sadness the muscles are floppy. In shame there is some defensive tension in some of the muscles, but not enough to hold the body in a tall proud posture.

5) **Body posture:** Shame often involves covering the face with a hand or hiding behind ones hair (hang one's head in shame). In guilt we see raised shoulders to make the head seem lower (a guilty shrug). Disgust has a particular twisted gait and eyes are averted. (He 'couldn't look at me' and 'turned away' in disgust.)

6) **Gesture:** Anger has numerous characteristic gestures such as finger-jabbing and shaking a fist. Joy promotes upward movements (jumping for joy).

7) **Voice tone:** Anger is uniformly firm, whereas disgust has a contemptuous voice tone with fluctuating emphasis, e.g. 'they gave me MASHED POTATO to eat, URGH, I could NOT eat THAT if you PAID me'. Sadness takes voice tone out of the mid-range, to either a high-pitched wail or to a

very low register. This change from the norm is designed to attract attention.

8) **Actions in the environment:** 'Cold shouldering' people when disgusted might involve not returning their calls, or not sitting next to them. Shame might involve doing your shopping in the late-night stores to avoid bumping into people you know. Jealous actions include checking your partner's phone when he or she is out.

9) **Interpretation or thought content:** Anxiety is characterised by a sharp focus on the feared event, and particularly what might go wrong, but with an absence of problem-solving. Anger is often accompanied by rehearsing over and over in one's mind the cause of the anger. In envy the person has compelling thoughts or images of the object of their desire. Linehan says, 'Emotions love themselves'. And so they bias your interpretations in their favour.

For certain emotions one of the domains, such as facial expression or body posture, may feature more prominently than others. Disgust, e.g. has a very distinctive facial feature, drawing the lip upwards on one side of the mouth, but has no obvious temperature change. Envy has tell-tale actions like making put-down remarks when someone shares a success. The heat generated in Anger is universally recognised, so much so that we say, 'cool it', when we want someone to down-regulate their anger.

One emotion at a time

People will often experience rapid-cycling between emotions. They tend to describe this as *'having lots of feelings at once'*. But in reality emotions don't co-exist. In skills training group I sometimes ask people to mimic the facial expression we'd see if they were both furiously angry and tragically sad at the same time. It is impossible to do, although it causes great hilarity as people attempt it.

Some clients are sceptical, saying that the 'face' exercise is unfair, as inside themselves they can feel both angry and sad. Again I would ask them to monitor their internal sensations while they conjure up that blend of those two emotions; being incandescent with rage and simultaneously heartbroken. They will usually acknowledge that they switch from one to the other rather than have both at once. They might notice that a mental image or thought goes with one of the emotions, e.g. *'How could my partner leave me in the lurch like that?'* leading to anger. A different thought such as *'I will really miss him'* is associated with sadness. Sometimes an emotion simply floods in before any thought, e.g. I was engulfed by a wave of sadness, and then I realised, *'he's not here.'* It is the ability of our body to change emotions very quickly that gives the impression that they are fused. Unfortunately therapists can unwittingly exacerbate the client's sense of feeling overwhelmed. Consider the following excerpt:

THERAPIST: You left the dinner table and went upstairs, what was the emotion?
CLIENT: I was furious with Carla for making those remarks
THERAPIST: And were you feeling anything else?
CLIENT: I guess a bit guilty that I had just stormed off...
THERAPIST: Any other emotions?
CLIENT: Er. maybe disgusted that she can even think I would lie to her?
THERAPIST: Is that all the emotions?
CLIENT: Um, perhaps I was scared that she would retaliate later...

Although all these emotions may have been valid, the way the therapist has asked about them is leading the client to believe that they happened at once, that it's possible to be simultaneously angry, guilty, disgusted, and afraid. Over-questioning can expound the myth that emotions arrive in one huge fog. Clients are often keen to please the therapist and will keep coming up with answers rather than genuinely tracking the thoughts and sensations that unfold moment by moment. My suggestion is to think more like an 'art dealer' during the assessment process, pouring over each painting, ascertaining its provenance and treating it with care before moving on to the next, rather than a 'market trader', asking, 'how many paintings have you got?' It is better to highlight the sequence of thoughts, sensations, and emotions than to create a list.

Clients may report feeling one emotion all the time, such as 'I always feel afraid' or 'Shame never goes away'. DBT helps clients to be mindful that their emotions come and go, like the weather. Over the course of a fortnight it might feel like it is always raining, but in fact there are showers, cloudy days, intermittent sun, and downpours. The illusion of constant rain is more likely if we see rain whenever we look out of the window. If you only glance outside once during the fortnight, then that shower you see represents 100% rain. Similarly clients might only notice unpleasant surges of emotion. So in effect, every time they check; Yep! there it is again, that horrible shame. To redress the balance, Linehan has a worksheet asking clients to record their emotions at regular intervals (Linehan 2015b pg 277).

It is possible that in the client's response repertoire one emotion fires up more quickly than the others. For example, if a client has had a lot of shame, the neurological architecture supporting a shame-response will be primed and ready to go with minimal prompts. As behaviourists we try not to get too distracted by the event in her history that caused her to be so shameful. We are more concerned with how the emotion shows up in the present moment. We accept that the physiology of the client, her previous patterns, and the environmental influences explain perfectly whatever emotion we see in front of us. And as we don't have a time machine to alter the past, we are very mindful of what we can do in the present. Just as when I call the breakdown service the mechanic is interested to hear that it was dark, the road unfenced, a deer ran out, my speed was too great to stop. But more importantly, how is the car malfunctioning? and what needs to be done to get it back on the road?

The difference between 'understandable' and 'appropriate' emotions

All emotions are understandable, even when we can't immediately see why, because every response has to have come from somewhere. But to regulate the emotion we need to work out what is roughly normal for that situation. When an emotional response is either too high, too low or very different to what is expected, we say it is dysregulated, i.e. it deviates from the norm. Here are two examples to share with clients. In both examples the emotion is fear.

Example 1. You and your friend have been invited to a party. Your friend tells you that as she won't be drinking she can drive you both there and back. However, at the end of the evening as you leave you realise she is so drunk she can hardly walk. You feel afraid to get in the car with her.

Example 2. You have been working on your social anxiety with a care worker, who has arranged for you to attend a day centre for people with similar issues. She has assured you everyone is friendly and says she will meet you inside. You reach the door but feel afraid to enter.

In the first example your fear fits the facts, it is telling you not to get in the car, because there is clear danger. The sensible thing to do is to obey the anxiety and call a taxi, using the emotion (unpleasant though it is) as a useful guide on how not to travel.

In the second example the fear is completely *understandable*, because meeting new people is potentially unpredictable and stressful, especially when you are out of practice. But there is no actual danger and so rather than obeying the emotion, you need to act opposite to any avoidant urges and go inside.

I use these examples because even adolescent clients grasp them easily – *don't get in the car, do go into the day centre*, the distinction is clear. But as they practise regulation skills they realise emotions are often hard to decipher, the dialectical influences on each moment are many, and the appropriate levels are not as obvious.

We also need to remember that sometimes the emotion needs up-regulating, rather than reducing, as in this incident:

> One client I worked with was living in supportive housing and had made friends with a new resident. The two girls had been out together a few times, to some music gigs. When my client could not find her denim jacket one day, she assumed she'd mislaid it while they were out. Her friend sympathised. Weeks later my client called round at her friend's flat unexpectedly, and there was the missing jacket on the bed. To cut a long story short, the girl had been stealing from her, not just the jacket but other smaller items that she had not even missed. When I enquired with my client whether she had been angry, she said, 'No, these things happen...'

I understood this response, because in my client's birth family her father had been so violent that if he ever got angry he would beat the children and their mother. Their fear of Dad's fury permeated all their interactions, such that no one was prepared to get even a little annoyed in case it set Dad off. Over time my client no longer felt any sensations that we would label as anger, she was so quick to bypass them. But where does that leave her if someone is stealing her things? What if she is unable to show even the slightest crossness in her tone of voice or facial expression? She becomes vulnerable to exploitation. Her empathic response does not fit the facts. If we decide to work on up-regulating the emotion then she doesn't have to get furious, but a certain firmness in tone, a seriousness of facial expression, is required to bring home that this is unacceptable behaviour.

What if the client doesn't want to change his or her emotional response? Then we move on to something they do want to work on. DBT therapists are technicians, helping clients to understand how to tweak their emotional plumbing to get the response they need. But even the most accomplished plumbers are not allowed to insist on mending your pipes. They need an invitation, and some collaboration from you. They might advise, in passing, that the cistern needs replacing, but it's your call. We present a rationale for anything we are offering to the client and then allow them to exercise their power of choice. But if they do choose to make changes, we know how they can go about it, outlined in Chapter 3.

References

Damasio, A. R. (1996). The somatic marker hypothesis and the possible functions of the prefrontal cortex. *Philosophical Transactions of the Royal Society of London. Series B: Biological Sciences, 351*(1346), 1413–1420.

LeDoux, J. E., & Pine, D. S. (2016). Using neuroscience to help understand fear and anxiety: A two-system framework. *American Journal of Psychiatry, 173*(11), 1083–1093.

Linehan, M. (2015b). *DBT Skills training handouts and worksheets*, 2nd ed. New York, London: Guilford Publications.

Torre, J. B., & Lieberman, M. D. (2018). Putting feelings into words: Affect labeling as implicit emotion regulation. *Emotion Review, 10*(2), 116–124.

The theory of 'opposite action'

The bi-directional nature of emotion components

In the last chapter I introduced the concepts of domains by which each emotion creates a unique signature in the body. To revise these again, they are:

- Temperature
- Facial expression
- Breathing
- Muscle tone
- Body posture
- Gesture
- Voice tone
- Actions in the environment
- Thought content

Every signature feature of the emotion adds to its momentum, in a snowball effect. Here is an illustration we might use to teach clients:

You live in a shared housing project. One morning you go to make a cup of coffee with the special (and very expensive) filter blend that you keep in a foil pack in the fridge. You find the pack is now almost empty, even though you only opened it yesterday.

Your immediate thought is, *someone has taken my coffee!* **(Interpretation)**

You frown and clench your jaw, your lips go into a thin line **(facial expression)**

Your shoulders and stomach tense, your heart rate quickens **(muscle tone)**

You breathe out sharply through your nose **(breathing)**

You feel hot **(temperature)**

You draw yourself up to your full height and put your hands on your hips **(posture)**

You proclaim loudly to another resident, "This packet was FULL yesterday." **(voice tone)**

You start jabbing your finger in the air, while you say, "Everyone KNOWS that coffee was mine." **(gesture)**

You put your cup pointedly back in the cupboard and slam the door. You jostle one of the other residents with your shoulder on the way past **(actions in the environment)**

The resident complains about you and you get a warning from staff.

The emotion is anger and each domain pushes it up the scale by one notch. The brain and body work in tandem, feeding back to each other. So as your brain reads each new feature it adds internal actions of its own; releasing hormones into your bloodstream, changing your temperature, and quickening your pulse. As you sense those internal adjustments you become even more tense and thus the spiral continues. This two-way effect helps emotion fire up really quickly; a fabulous advantage in escaping predators, but not so useful in coffee-related incidents.

Fortunately the bi-directional nature of these changes means that to bring the emotion down, we just reverse the effects in each domain. If you take *opposite actions* to the anger by lowering your temperature, relaxing your muscles, dropping your arms down, smoothing out your face, unclenching your jaw, etc., then each step will reduce the emotional intensity by a small amount. This process is dialectical, in that there is no single action you can take to regulate every emotion. For example, telling people to take a deep breath will reduce anxiety or anger, but not if the emotion is sadness, when the breath is already elongated. Getting people to 'cool off outside' helps if the emotion is anger, but if the person is terrified they are already cold.

To demonstrate the power of opposite action we often do this exercise in skills training group:

> **First instruction:** Let's pretend that someone in this room is our long lost friend and we had no idea they were going to be here today, we are going to greet them in a way that shows how thrilled we are to see them, GO! (Don't give people too much time to think about it, just encourage them to throw themselves into it, only for a couple of minutes.)
>
> **Second instruction:** Ok, now let's do exactly the same thing again, the same words in the same voice, same gestures, same smile, same movements. But we are also going to do just one tiny part of *acting opposite* to joy; we are going to keep our eyebrows down. Just that. Keep everything else the same.

The effect of changing this one domain (facial expression) is huge. Typical responses are: "it feels fake," "I can't get my voice as high," and "I just don't feel as happy." This is a great demonstration to foster confidence in the skill because the reduction in the sensation of pleasure is so dramatic. (As an aside, if someone doesn't eyebrow-flash you on greeting, they're either not that pleased to see you or they have had Botox.) After the exercise ask this question: "If you can get that much reduction by acting opposite in just one domain, what do you think happens when you add the others in?"

Behavioural chain and solution analysis

Clients might assume, 'Great, I have problems with anger, so I can just act opposite all the time, keep myself cool, make sure I don't frown, slow my breathing, relax my muscles...' But that would be a non-dialectical approach, failing to allow that sometimes the anger is valid. This is why in DBT we only regulate an emotion that played a significant part in the chain of events leading to one of those unwanted behaviours we are tracking on the diary card (an internet search for 'DBT diary cards' will throw up a great selection of cards that can be used in different settings). Usually these cards will be used to track self-harm incidents, suicidal actions, or urges to do these things. However, as DBT has advanced from treating BPD the behaviours might include disordered eating (e.g. bingeing, purging, or missing meals), substance misuse, offending behaviours, and problems associated with adolescence (e.g. missing school, absconding, under-age behaviours).

In the coffee scenario above, the client was tracking behaviours that could lead to eviction. The target was not 'getting angry' – it's fine to be angry about having your goods stolen. But pushing another resident threatened our client's continued residence in her accommodation, so this was the target behaviour. Once we have got our target – the push – we will then run a behavioural analysis, which means dissecting the sequence of events in freeze-frame, so we can tell exactly when and how the emotion pops up. Reducing the emotion is only relevant in order to avoid the push, and our client can probably agree to that. This is a completely different approach than saying, "your anger is out of control, let's work on that." As a therapist it's my job to show how regulating an emotion in a given context is meaningful to the client's goals for a life worth living.

'Pinpoints of time' are everything in DBT. If the client cuts herself three times on a Tuesday, with the same knife in the same room, then for the purpose of chain analysis these would be considered as three separate incidents. For any target behaviour the therapist will enquire, "What time did that happen?" "Where were you?" "What was happening just before?" "What happened just after?" Because if we don't know the exact context how could we say whether or not the emotion fitted the facts?

Below is an example chain of a behaviour that has been targeted for reduction, in this case a self-harm action of pinching the skin. The client is a 24-year-old woman who has ended up temporarily residing with her mother after a relationship break-up. She is having to sleep on the sofa because it is such a small flat. This target incident happened at 09:40 on a Thursday morning. The client was still in bed in the living room (Table 3.1).

If the therapists had requested a narrative version of what happened the client might have said, "I pinched myself because I had a row with my mother, she had a right go at me for laying in bed, and I hate living there." She might say, "I just feel bad" or even more vague: "I pinched myself because I've had a bad morning." It is only in tracking the incremental changes during the incident that we can follow her rollercoaster ride. However, the chain is short – it helps us know where to intervene, it is not the treatment in itself.

So let's explore our chain of events. In the initial response the client noticed being angry *before* she had any discernible thoughts. It is entirely possible for a stimulus such as a harsh

Table 3.1 Chain analysis of self-harm behaviour

Type of link	Sequence of events
Event	Mum came in and said (in a harsh tone), "get up and clear up this mess"
Emotion	Anger 5/10
Thought	She speaks to me like I'm a dog
Action	Shouts, "Don't snap at me like that, I'll do it when I'm ready"
Event	Mum turns away and goes into the kitchen
Thought	Now I've upset her
Emotion	Guilt 4/10
Thought	I can't do anything right. That's why I am on my own
Emotion	Sadness 8/10
Sensation	Feels pricking behind her eyes
Action	Grabs her upper arm and pinches herself really hard, focusses on the pain
Action	Takes a sharp intake of breath
Sensation	Stops feeling the urge to cry

tone to produce defensive anger, which she then justifies by saying to herself, "She speaks to me like I'm a dog." In DBT we do not automatically assume that the cognition preceded the emotion. But it was when the thought 'that's why I am on my own' came into her mind that the highest emotion occurred, and she harmed herself. The sadness was undoubtedly appropriate, and nobody wants to find themselves sofa-surfing because of a break-up. The harsh retort from Mum probably slammed this home. A sharp intake of breath is opposite to the long sighs of sadness, so maybe pinching herself regulated the sadness downwards by producing a physiological change in her body. However, the sadness itself might have been a regulatory mechanism for guilt, diverting her attention away from how she was mean to her Mum. Over time we might notice if there is a pattern that when the client feels guilty she escapes into feeling sad about her situation.

Each emotion in the chain has factors that would pump it up, and others that would deflate it, which is how dialectical tensions push and pull us around, making it hard to decide how much is too much and how much is insufficient:

Anger: Justification: Not being allowed to sleep in, being woken to a harsh tone, not being given a chance to tidy before the rebuke. Mitigating factors: Mum has been generous, the space is limited.

Guilt: Justification: It's not acceptable to snap at older people, parents, people offering you accommodation. Mitigating factors: The mess might not have been intentional, if there are no wardrobes or drawers to tidy into.

Sadness: Justification: Loss of own accommodation, loss of partnership status. Lack of supportive comments from her mother. Mitigating factors: Mum is offering a sofa at a time of need

Clients with emotion regulation difficulties find it hard to separate emotions, to appreciate the validity in them or to work out how they might be expressed and solved. They may judge themselves or others, seeking to establish who is right and who is wrong, rather than seeing this complex web of dialectical tensions. When emotions flip rapidly they can experience them as overwhelming and it is the job of the therapist to unravel the knot into a sequential thread.

Why analyse past events?

Whatever psychological theory we espouse, whether it be Attachment Theory, Relational Frame Theory, Psychodynamics, or Transactional Analysis it will definitely explain a client's actions perfectly *in retrospect*. But there is only one reliable predictor of future behaviour: Past behaviour. The best guess we can make of what any person will do is to look at what they've done before.

Clients therefore are less likely to use skills because they don't have a history of doing so. And as I mentioned previously, we don't have a time machine, so there's not much we can do about that. Or is there?

The process of chain and solution analysis takes advantage of the capacity of the human brain to create mental models, i.e. *imagined reconstructions* of the event under scrutiny. This facility allows us to mock-up, re-run, test out, and troubleshoot new ways for the client to approach that situation and is the nearest thing we've got to that time machine. The function is to give us rich contextual data for that behavioural rehearsal. By activating behaviour we are creating new neural networks that underpin the revisions, almost like laying down an alternative past. If we do this 'action replay' often enough the client will strengthen the new responses, making the skilful behaviour more likely to play out in vivo.

Remember the contextual data is key. Let's imagine a client got very angry when asking for a change of medication from his psychiatrist. If we were to forget our 'time machine' strategy we might just say "why don't we rehearse how to approach the psychiatrist the next time you meet?" The trouble is we're likely to miss some of the controlling variables; perhaps there was an unanswered phone ringing in an adjoining room; the client hadn't eaten; their shoes were pinching. Perhaps it was a certain look or tone that pushed the client's buttons, and they would need to be able to tolerate that next time round. By sticking closely to what actually happened, we have more data about the peripheral factors, those outside the client's awareness that nevertheless played a part in the outcome. If we focus on a future event we can only guess what might occur, and we're not likely to think of things like the sound of the phone ringing.

I remember once having a client who went into hospital for a hysterectomy, which produced some poignant and painful triggers for her, and she ended up harming herself on the ward.

On chaining this afterwards I thought we should rehearse skills for coping with future triggers of a similar sort. I was having supervision with Heidi Heard at the time and she pulled me up on this, insisting I regulate the emotions that cropped up specifically related to the hysterectomy. I pointed out,

> "Heidi, you know a hysterectomy is a one-time deal, right?"
> "Trust the process," She replied, "Just trust the process."

It was only then that I fully appreciated the importance of modelling that alternative past. After our rehearsal, those remembered contextual factors plus our new skills almost create an illusion for the client that they did indeed do it differently. We are changing history in the neural architecture of the brain.

When I am listening to tapes for supervision I can tell if a therapist has not quite grasped this concept – that the function of the session is to lay down a new history – because they keep asking for more and more links in the chain, without solving any of them. It is wishful thinking that the client's insight alone will provide the required change; that if the client can just understand *why* they get angry, or that there was some guilt lurking around, or if they can only see how they were avoiding sadness, this will be enough. But by the time clients get into DBT we know insight alone is not the answer. Most had on average 15 years of treatments before coming to our service, with excellent clinicians. They knew what trauma caused their responses, what triggers maintained them and how devastating the consequences can be. They just wanted to know how to make it all stop. In short they needed practice in doing it differently.

There is one more obstacle to coaching emotion regulation, and that is the intoxicating attraction to both clients and professionals of those Distress Tolerance skills that I mentioned in the introduction. Let's imagine that you have had chronic back pain for a year, and your doctor says she is referring you to a programme called 'Back Pain Tolerance'. What is she telling you about your back pain? That it's not going down any time soon, right? Yet there's a collective delusion around the Distress Tolerance skills, that they will relieve distress. I always remind group leaders to point out that Linehan named that module very well, Distress Tolerance is for getting through without making things worse. It is not a change strategy, but falls at the *acceptance* end of DBT.

In fairness to DBT therapists, it might be because the skills in this module are laid out in handy lists that they often coach them in preference emotion regulation. They only have to enquire, "Were you distressed?" (and which client is going to say no?) to legitimise going down that route. As a consultant, when I get asked about a client who is not improving in DBT I can almost predict that they will be over-relying on Distress Tolerance, and have probably had minimal coaching in emotional literacy. Listening to supervision recordings I sometimes hear a therapist say clearly to the client, "I think we need to rehearse some Emotion Regulation skills" (which has me beaming in delight…), then they move straight into coaching distraction (☹).

Unfortunately the client who deals with emotion by distracting, whether with mindful colouring or counting their breath, is simply at the mercy of time passing, hoping that if they ignore the trigger for long enough the emotion will go away. Some things will. If your distress is caused by New Year fireworks keeping you up all night, tolerance is fine. But if you are sad because you are sleeping on your Mum's sofa and you really long for a place of your own, you have to acknowledge that loss and start solving it. Or if you feel guilty for snapping at her, you need to make a repair. Or if you feel angry that she hasn't appreciated your difficulties and her harsh tone hurt your feelings, then you need to pick an appropriate moment, sit down with her and have that conversation. Of course you also need to see Mum's side of it, but you cannot simply distract yourself out of these problems.

DBT is a holistic approach but occasionally gets a reputation for being formulaic. I believe that comes from the over-coaching of Distress Tolerance skills, and particularly if the instructions are trotted out to the client without contextualising the distress; feeling sad? Watch a happy film! Feeling lonely? Walk a neighbour's dog! Feeling angry? Play your favourite tracks! These are non-dialectical suggestions, implying that one size fits all and leaving clients feeling misunderstood.

There is a place for tolerating distress. For example if I am stuck in a 20 mile traffic jam and it's not moving, I might as well turn on the radio. In fact distraction skills are perfect if I am forced into any painful waiting period. Acceptance skills are excellent for anything that despite my best efforts I cannot change, e.g. the highways department have built a motorway at the end of my garden. Lastly, if my emotion is so high that I lose access to my rational mind, then physiological and grounding strategies can provide a bridge to my emotion regulation skills.

Emotion
validation

Obtaining an 'invitation to treat'

There are three essential components to the skill of opposite action when regulating emotion. They are validation, validation, and validation. There is no emotional literacy without acceptance that something in the emotional experience has value. Unless we are to continue as part of the invalidating environment, we must first, reliably and accurately align ourselves not with the change end of the dialectic, but with the bit of the emotion, however small, that actually fits the facts.

Because emotional responses are such an important part of a person's identity, therapists need an *invitation to treat* whenever an emotion is to be regulated. After all, in normal life people can be as emotional as they wish, as long as they remain within the law. A client simply turning up to therapy does not give a mental health professional permission to ride roughshod over their natural reactions. DBT sometimes gets a bad name as harsh or punitive, and in my view this is always when the therapy team underestimate the level of validation and collaboration required. The role of therapist in DBT is much like a personal shopper. We may advise, but the final say lies with the client.

This is the route to strengthening the sense of self they need to develop so they can trust in their emotional experiences.

A young man referred to me was preceded by communications from both his parent and GP stating that he was an academic superstar who must be well enough to take up the wonderful place he had been offered in a top-tier university. Of course the first words out of his mouth when he arrived were 'I'm never going back into academia'. My job was to help him achieve his stated aim, to quit study, without having his parents and associates on his back.

In Marsha's metaphor of learning to pitch a tent, emotion validation is preparing the ground. Let's go back to our example of the empty coffee packet. If after hearing about the incident from the client I immediately hone in on reducing her anger, I am pretty sure she would take a dim view of both DBT and me. From her perspective she has good reason to be angry – she was looking forward to her coffee and didn't get it, because someone had taken her property without asking. The anger acts as confirmation that she has been offended (which is true) so it is self-validating. She won't welcome me wading in with instructions for how to get it down. Even if her angry outbursts are threatening her accommodation, pointing this out before laying the groundwork will fracture our alliance. I need an *invitation* to offer change. Linehan suggests we should look for the nugget of truth in the client's response *before* working on the problematic part of it.

THERAPIST: Oh no, was it the coffee you brought in here last week, in your flask? It smelt amazing. *(T. validates the value of what was lost.)*

CLIENT: Yes it's a special blend, I order it online.

THERAPIST: … and once you get used to a blend you can't just go back to instant coffee. And it was all gone? *(T. is using two types of validation – one is affirming the awfulness of* *the experience, and the second, actively inviting the client to repeat the key point, confirming that it has been heard. The therapist is <u>not</u> checking, 'are you quite sure the pack was empty?')*

CLIENT: Well a few grains were left in the bottom. And it's the principle of the thing, if whoever it was had asked then I would have given them some.

THERAPIST: I know you would, it's a liberty to just take stuff without asking. And the person you pushed, was that who you suspected had taken it? *(T. Provides normative validation. T. also seeks clarification. Again, this is not to check the facts, but more to communicate 'I need to make sure I've got a good picture of this'.)*

CLIENT: Not really. I have no idea who took it. She was just in my way.

THERAPIST: That makes sense, anger flares up when we get blocked, so first you wanted the coffee and then you wanted to get out. Both blocked – a double trigger! *(T. teaches about the situations in which anger fits the facts for anger.)*

CLIENT: And now because of that I am the one with a black mark against me.

THERAPIST: Yes that's upsetting. Maybe if we could have got the anger down a bit about the empty packet, the pushing might not have happened. But we wouldn't want to take it down too far, because you had good reason to be angry. Just enough so you don't have any extra problems to deal with. Then we need to work out how to communicate that people should *ask* if they want to try your coffee and not just take it. It's perfectly reasonable to want to keep hold of what's yours. *(T. validates the distress and introduces the concept of dialectics – the anger itself was valid but the level was too high. T. addresses the function of the emotion, to communicate to others what was unacceptable.)*

CLIENT: They won't listen.

THERAPIST: Maybe not, that's always a risk. I guess it might not make any difference whatever we do (contemplative pause.) And at the same time, it doesn't feel fair if you don't get your say about people taking your stuff. *(T. validates the client's worry that change would be ineffective, using not only verbal validation but pausing to give genuine consideration of the point. Then T. adds further validation of the client's loss.)*

CLIENT: True.

THERAPIST: We could give it a go and see how it feels, see if we can get the pitch right? *(T. seeks an invitation to treat.)*

CLIENT: You're right, it's not fair if I am the one who looks like the bad guy.

THERAPIST: Exactly. I'm sure I can help with this. *(T. validates their agreement, based on the client's goals. Using the phrase 'I can help' underscores that the client is leading the direction.)*

It would be much quicker to start with something like, 'looking at our chain the problem was when you pushed that other resident. It seems anger was the key there, so how about we work on getting that anger down?' But this immediately puts the client on the back foot, perhaps even eliciting shame. The work the therapist did on validating was what made the change intervention palatable to the client, who already feels aggrieved. A few extra moments to seek out the nugget of truth in the anger, and get an invitation to treat made all the difference.

Consider the example from Chapter 3 where the mother had spoken harshly to her sofa-surfing daughter.

Example A – Adequate Validation

THERAPIST: So the first thing you heard was your mum telling you to get up and clear up the mess?

CLIENT: It was her tone that really annoyed me.

THERAPIST: It must have been a shock to wake up to that? You had no time to even think of how to respond. I hate it myself if I'm taken by surprise.

CLIENT: Yes I really didn't see that coming.

THERAPIST: And then your physiology just kicks in automatically…

CLIENT: That's so true! My heart was pounding.

THERAPIST: And I'm sure that must have played a part in your reply

CLIENT: It did! Though I felt bad afterwards.

THERAPIST: Yeah, you mentioned that. What do you think was the part you felt bad about?

CLIENT: Snapping at her I guess, it is so cramped with both of us living there.

Here the client is not defensive as the emotion has been validated. Let's contrast that with a well-meaning but less validating response:

Example B – Inadequate Validation

THERAPIST: So you woke up to your mum telling you to get up and clear up the mess?

CLIENT: It was her tone that really annoyed me.

THERAPIST: (Kindly) Maybe she was expressing her frustration at the mess, rather than at you?

CLIENT: Well she could have just said it politely, or let me wake up properly first

THERAPIST: I guess it's hard when there's such a small space

CLIENT: I realise that. It's not like I *intended* to be sleeping on her sofa.

THERAPIST: (Soothing tone) Of course you didn't. I'm only suggesting that she might not have meant it to come across so sharply, after all she readily let you stay, she must care at some level.

CLIENT: I never said she didn't care, do you think I'm ungrateful?

THERAPIST: No, not at all! I didn't mean to imply that. I was just trying to be dialectical, and see it from both sides. And then we can work out whether your anger fitted the facts?

CLIENT: Look, I KNOW she's frustrated. We both are. I'm not saying she was wrong, I'm saying I didn't like her tone. And you're right, my emotion DIDN'T fit the facts. I always get it wrong, that's why I'm here. isn't it? You don't need to rub my nose in it.

In example B the therapist misses out validating the anger, and goes straight into perfectly reasonable change strategies – taking a dialectical position and checking if the emotion fitted the facts. Both interventions fit very well with the DBT model, but without validation the client becomes defensive. Although there are areas of agreement she responds as though she is being corrected. The therapist can tell something is wrong, but any attempt to pull it back falls flat. Sadly this type of exchange can lead to the client being labelled as prickly. The therapist may be *intending* to soothe the client; conveying the message, 'Your Mum probably didn't mean to be offensive, she must want you around. She cares about you'. But the comments were not perceived that way because they contained the underlying message; *you had no reason to feel angry*. My top tip is as soon as you have got the chain, if there is an emotion, ask yourself, 'what can I possibly validate here?' Remember that validation is not praise, it is showing how something makes sense. It is paving the path to your invitation to treat.

Lack of validation is so frequently associated with resistance in therapy, that if ever I notice that 'tug-of-war' sensation during a session, I stop and say something like, 'I wonder if I have actually been validating enough, here? I don't think I've acknowledged just how it must have been for you in that moment'.

The client is much more likely to cooperate in down-regulating the intensity of an emotion if the therapist starts by looking at how to problem-solve the valid part of it. However, there are a couple of problems that get in the way – the first is when the client can't identify the emotion, and the second when the emotion is missing, and needs to be up-regulated rather than down-regulated.

When the client can't identify an emotion

If a client's early education was devoid of any information on emotions, they might only be aware of three feeling states; miserable, happy, and ok. As an initial intervention you might ask them to check in with their body every hour and just record what they notice. They can then refer to Emotion regulation handout number 6 on pages 214–223 of Linehan's *DBT Skills training handouts and worksheets* (2015b), which offers a guide to identifying each of the big emotion families. For example, in the section on anger there are:

- Words that are associated with anger
- Prompting events for feeling angry
- Common interpretations leading to anger
- Biological changes that happen when you are angry
- Expressions and actions associated with anger
- Aftereffects of feeling angry.

Advise the client, 'If you can't identify what you are feeling, get this list out and go through it until you recognise something'. For clients who have more limited learning abilities Julie Brown (2015) has also adapted some of the materials in her Skills System manual, see the list of references at the end of this book. I am aware that there are resources such as the 'feeling wheel' which goes into much more nuanced descriptions, but my top tip is to start with a smaller palette of emotions.

One of my clients was a businessman whose lack of emotion had served him well at work, but was causing problems in his social life. He was sceptical that attending to feelings would have any value, and referred to any unpleasant internal sensations as 'stress'. At the conclusion of a work meeting one day he noticed he was 'not feeling right'. He remained in his chair and went back over the paperwork. This time he noticed a clause that he had skimmed over, assuming it was irrelevant to his department. On reflection he realised there were hidden implications. He was genuinely surprised that he had responded viscerally to something that he had barely registered cognitively. After that he was much more willing to consider his emotions, even if he did not like them. Noting that on this occasion anxiety helped him was the turning point.

In our NHS Trust we often invited clients who had been through the DBT programme to participate in staff training. One of my ex-clients was asked, 'Don't you become dependent on your DBT therapist? How do you cope when therapy ends?' to which she replied, 'Whenever I have an emotion I just chain it myself'. By this she meant that she could look back over the context (as I outlined in Chapter 3); identify the emotion; discern what it was telling her; decide whether it was a good fit for the circumstances; and then alter the level up or down as needed.

These strategies will generally help where a client notices they are experiencing *something* in their body. Other clients, though, can complain of being emotionally numb.

Here is an example;

THERAPIST: So this weekend your daughter was back from France and was bringing her new partner for lunch so you could meet him?

CLIENT: I hadn't seen her for six months, and, you know, I wanted to make a good impression on her new man. I spent all day Friday cooking, but I don't mind that. At least I have plenty of food in now.

THERAPIST: They did come?

CLIENT: Well, they got here late, and, you know, young people are busy. They didn't have time to eat, just popped in really. For about ten minutes.

THERAPIST: Oh, dear, that must have been disappointing?

CLIENT: Not really, I haven't seen her for ages, so what's another weekend? I'm not sure when I will see her now, but, ah well, that's ok. (Picks some fluff off her skirt.)

THERAPIST: I guess you have kind of got used to her being away. And at the same time, you had suffered a loss. When they left, what did you notice in yourself?

CLIENT: Nothing, they'd already eaten, so I thought I might as well have some of the food.

THERAPIST: You didn't notice any thoughts or emotions?

CLIENT: No, I just went in the kitchen, to get one of my ordinary dinner plates, I didn't want to use the best ones, because it was only me. Then I had this real craving for a gin and tonic, and that's how I ended up drinking all evening.

In this scenario it looks as though any emotion of sadness (disappointment, feeling let down) is completely absent. Linehan cautions against interpreting the client's internal experience. This would include making assumptions that the client is supressing, denying, or deliberately downplaying her response to elicit sympathy. Behaviours like looking down at her skirt or making verbal denials can be misinterpreted, because therapists with easy action to emotions may not be able to believe that sadness is not intensely present. Yet the sensations associated with sadness may have been so aversive in the past that the client automatically bypasses that system response altogether. If she says she didn't feel sad, believe her. It is invalidating to do otherwise.

A more useful approach is to highlight that in this situation many people *might* feel disappointed, which is in the sadness family. At this point we are describing a construct rather than creating a feeling. We educate the client that sadness would function to honour the loss she had suffered. Being tearful or speaking in a sad tone would alert others to help, or just motivate her to self-soothe. We could float the hypothesis that the gin and tonic is a form of comfort-seeking, and wonder at whether, if she were to act as if she were sad instead, those urges might go down. We could gently review the benefits of letting her daughter know she was sad. All this is approached in the interests of experimentation, we cannot drag people kicking and screaming into having emotions, let alone loving them.

I just referred to this process as 'describing a construct' and this is a good place for me to reference the work of prolific researcher Lisa F. Barrett (2017), who has been exploring emotional responses in the brain under laboratory conditions for around 20 years. Her findings suggest that there are no 'fingerprints' or 'barcodes' of emotions that remain lodged in the brain or body. We cannot say *this sequence is anger, and this one is sadness.* In fact there are NO unique characteristics of any emotion at all. We can cry when we are happy or when we're sad. We can shout for joy or in anger. We can hide in shame or in fear. So anger in one person may be expressed and experienced in a more muted form than in another. It is only anger because we mutually recognise it as such.

This is why I have chosen my words carefully when writing about emotions. I refer to 'signatures' or 'signature features'. Your written signature shares some characteristics of emotion; you have to create it afresh each time it is needed, from letters that you also use in other words. Each example of your signature will be subtly different depending on how rushed or tired you are, the pen you use, or the paper you write on. Yet it is still recognisable. Emotions are not systems lodged in your brain waiting to come out, they are sequences that overlap, fire up, and dissipate moment by moment. And they are different in everyone. In my family, when I am in a rage I am vocal. My husband by contrast has only one symptom of fury; a barely noticeable nostril flare. I am quicker to rile and it blows over rapidly. My husband is very even-tempered so those rare nostril-flaring situations take longer to soothe, probably because he has a lot less practice at dealing with this anomaly. Neither of us knows what the other feels inside, we can only guess.

So when we are coaching clients who under-emote, we might not be causing them to 'feel' anything different. Instead, we are nudging their reactions closer to what is socially expected, bearing in mind that each emotion serves a function, and without that the person may be at a disadvantage. Emotions communicate to others and to ourselves, and yet we also have to consider that they are painful. We're not here to make our clients' lives worse, so we need to test out in each context whether the emotion might be helpful. We sometimes advise, 'fake it till you make it', because when an emotion is missing it takes some time to develop a new system response, internally and externally. Even then, if we are up-regulating sadness, will the person feel what I feel when I am sad? Who knows? Maybe no two people ever feel the same. All we can hope is that they might do more problem-solving, receive more empathy from others, and have less discomfort in the longer term if their reactions are more socially recognisable. It's not a given – it depends. In Chapter 6 I give an example of up-regulating sadness, so you can see how it would look in-session.

As a further resource for identifying emotions, Section B of this book describes features of emotions that can be used in educating the client. The ultimate aim is that when they have an emotion they experience the following responses:

1) I know what this experience is

2) I trust it didn't just come from nowhere

3) I have some curiosity about what it is trying to tell me

4) I know what to do if it fits the facts

5) I am pretty sure I can increase or decrease it if I need to.

The zero option

This whole chapter has been about validating emotion, so you might wonder if there is ever a situation where the emotion is not valid at all, where we would have to down-regulate all the way to zero? There are some examples, but they are not that common.

Let's take fear of spiders:

- If I am in Australia and see a spider – my fear fits the facts as it could be deadly.

- If I am weeding my flowerbeds in the UK and see a spider – it can still give a nasty bite, so at a much lower level fear would still fit the facts.

- If I am indoors and out of the corner of my eye see a piece of wool on the carpet that *reminds* me of a spider – there is no danger whatsoever so I can down-regulate my fear to zero.

Unfortunately, the idea of reducing emotions to zero is tempting to mental health professionals and clients alike; clients, because their hurt feelings stay around for a long time. Staff members because they want to reduce distress for people in their care, especially where high emotion has been paired with risky be-haviour. Getting rid of the emotion becomes synonymous with eliminating risk. Any valuable emotional messages take a back seat in favour of keeping the client safe.

An adult client was estranged from her family and in hos-pital over her birthday. She complained to the staff that her mother had not even sent a card, and her face fell.

The nurse told her,

But just look at all the other cards, do see how many people care about you? And we are getting pizzas in to-night. We can have a celebration with your friends here on the ward! Come on let's paint your nails so they'll look lovely.

This response made complete sense, because the client regularly engaged in highly suicidal behaviours and was on a high obser-vation level. Staff were worried about what she could do to her-self, and the implications for the unit if there were a suicide on the ward. It would seem unkind to leave the patient feeling sad on her birthday. These are all excellent reasons to down-regulate the emotion, but if it fits the facts it has to be addressed.

In the next chapter we will look at solutions for valid emotions.

References

Barrett, L. F. (2017). *How emotions are made: The secret life of the brain*. Boston, MA: Houghton Mifflin Harcourt.

Brown, J. F. (2015). *The Emotion Regulation Skills System for Cognitively Challenged Clients: A DBT-Informed Approach*. New York, London: Guilford Publications.

Linehan, M. (2015b). *DBT Skills training handouts and worksheets*, 2nd ed. New York, London: Guilford Publications.

CHAPTER

5

Problem-solving

When I mention that problem-solving is an emotion-regulation strategy therapists sometimes do a double-take, because it's so obvious AND so forgettable! If you are fearful because your garden fence blew down and you are worried your dog will escape, then mending the fence will reduce that anxiety. If you feel guilty that you haven't visited your elderly grandmother for weeks so you decide to pop round to see her, your guilt will go down. These are the purest, most authentic emotion regulation strategies for valid emotions. Unfortunately there are a number of obstacles to this problem-solving process in clients with severely suicidal behaviour.

1) **Depleted resources.** Exhausted by emotional pain from life events, clients may have tried solutions that have failed through no fault of their own. They have been beset by bad luck, abuse, neglect, or had a succession of disappointments. They bounce between wanting to die and fighting to stay alive – both of which are physically taxing. They have no motivation to self-care, and yet require increased rest and nutrients to repair from self-harm injuries.

2) **Cognitive impairment.** Once clients have decided that suicide is their best option they stop exercising their mental muscles, because being dead will render all other solutions

unnecessary. Clients and therapists often overlook the mental incapacity caused by self-injury. We wouldn't expect people to make important decisions immediately after a tooth extraction, or a knee replacement, or a bad fall. And if they were forced to do so, we'd understand that they were not at their most clear-headed. Self-harm is a physical shock to the body.

3) **Distracted by risk.** Everyone wants to keep the client safe from self-harm or suicide, so much so that the trigger problem can be sidelined. One of the most risky emotions, in my view, is pervasive disappointment. Clients' dashed expectations can be excruciatingly painful, especially when comparing themselves to peers. They then self-invalidate because this doesn't seem like a 'good enough' reason for suffering. Their therapist might also reassure them that such comparisons don't matter and what really matters is not dying. Clients themselves complain, 'When I stop being suicidal, everyone thinks I'm ok'. When in fact their unsolved disappointment inevitably returns until they have some achievements to be pleased about.

4) **Problem magnitude.** Related to the previous factor, people who fear disappointment are not going to sign up for more. If where they are now is too far from where they want to go they will balk at taking even the first step. It can be hard to motivate problem-solving without the client perceiving this as pressure. The dialectical movements between acceptance and change are particularly helpful here.

Some emotions are related to larger life problems, such as being unhappy at work, living in poor accommodation, being estranged from family, having identity issues, or being beset by financial problems. These cannot be solved in one session, so you might need to introduce an additional diary card (running alongside the standard card) specifically to monitor the steps towards that bigger goal. I call this 'simultaneous tracking', because it enables the therapist to keep tabs on efforts to solve those long-term issues. For example clients seeking employment may record their job search activities, people wanting to get fitter might be tracking their exercise, and people with no life goals might collect information about their research activities.

My advice is to introduce the second card carefully. It is not designed to put pressure on the client, but may be perceived that way. You might say,

> This problem is worth tracking because the current situation is making you miserable. I don't want to forget that alongside the work we are doing on your (self-harming) we are also trying to get your life back on track, and you deserve every bit of help I can give with that.

I have provided an example of a diary card for tracking progress on increasing social contacts (Table 5.1).

I chose this example because so many of our DBT clients are chronically lonely, and rely on paid professionals for solace. No wonder, given that relationships are the source of much emotional pain. After a while they lose self-confidence, perhaps believing it will be impossible to make personal relationships outside of a clinical context. Therapists can 'catch' this hopelessness and assume that a client will never have an intimate relationship or the kind of friends they might go on holiday with. Clients remain stuck in this position because they'd rather cope with being alone than run the gauntlet of possible rejection.

Even more common is relational disappointment, where the client is dissatisfied with their partner but fears the cliff-edge of separating. Listening to session recordings I often reflect to the therapist, 'It sounds as though this client is really unhappy in her relationship?' To which they reply, 'Yes, she doesn't get on with (him or her) at all, but she can't leave because... *(the partner*

Table 5.1 Second diary card to track friend-recruiting behaviours

Progress on goal to get more social contacts	Mon	Tues	Wed	Thur	Fri	Sat	Sun	Commitment to do it (%)	Degree of difficulty %	What helped?
Message lapsed friend										
Send card/notelet to old friend										
Review social media for supportive groups & join										
Research local hobby/social clubs										
Email group organisers										
Say hi to a vague acquaintance										
Turn up to a new activity										
Make small talk with a new person										
Ask what people do for leisure locally										
Give number & suggest coffee										
Join specific groups for meet-ups (dating/ friendship)										
Respond to enquiries										
Visit a café and get to know staff/regulars										
Host a McMillan or similar (Tupperware, chocolate sales, etc.) event at home										
Offer to help out a neighbour										
Organise a trip out to a cinema/theatre/ countryside ramble, etc.										
Volunteer at a charity/church										
Invite someone out										
Accept invitations										

is the carer; they have kids; she has nowhere to go; there are financial reasons; etc)'. It's often a quandary for the client; Am I unhappy because I am unwell? Or am I unwell because I am unhappy? A dialectical approach would suggest it is somewhere in the middle. Fear of client instability after a break-up can bias helpers towards maintaining the status quo. But unresolved relationship issues rumble around like an unexploded bomb. Paradoxically, helping a client solve the practicalities of separating can release the pressure valve, even if they stay.

To therapists I say ignore these big-ticket items at your peril. If at the start of treatment the client is lonely, or feels trapped in a relationship, or is terminally bored by their daily routine, and they are still in the same place at the end, no amount of opposite action will effect a cure. This is exactly what Linehan means when she says that the true goal of DBT for suicidal patients is to create a life worth living. And at the same time, the client needs emotion regulation skills to tolerate the feelings that come up at each new step.

Increasing problem-solving behaviour

In supervision I notice that therapists often underestimate the level of detail required to activate behaviour, the following examples show first low then high focus on potential obstacles.

Solution generation session A

THERAPIST: Sounds like you need some kind of hobby. Can you think of anything you might like to do, or have done before, what interests you?

CLIENT: Not really... erm... I used to play badminton at university.

THERAPIST: I think there are some clubs locally where you can just turn up to mix-in sessions, how about joining one of those?

CLIENT: Yes, I suppose so.

THERAPIST: OK, we can put it on the list anyway. Anything else?

CLIENT: I like reading.

THERAPIST: The library has a list of book groups, so there is bound to be one covering your area. Let's add that too.

This is a great start, but more is needed, specifically detailed trouble-shooting and commitment, which in my view have the most influence over the outcome.

Solution generation example B

THERAPIST: You mentioned badminton, did you know there's a mix-in session at Bispham leisure centre on Thursdays, 7pm till 9pm. Here is the leaflet... But do you still have a racket?

CLIENT: I think there's one in the garage. Not sure what state it's in, though.

THERAPIST: If that one's a bit ropey what would you do, would you want to buy a new one?

CLIENT: Maybe, I haven't played for ages... so, um, I don't know.

THERAPIST: Yes, I know what you mean, especially as this club might not suit you. I wonder if at Bispham you can see into the courts, without having to commit to playing? You know, if you just happened to wander through on Thursday and got to check it out without having to join. Do they have a viewing gallery there?

CLIENT: I don't know, but I like the idea of snooping around a bit. I'm pretty sure you pass the badminton courts to get to the café. I might even be able to see in from outside. Do I sound really cowardly?

THERAPIST: Who cares? If it helps you feel more comfortable, I'm all for it. If they are all pensioners or 16-year-olds you might not want to join, and if they are Olympic standard, let's find somewhere else...

CLIENT: But even if they seem ok, I will be the rusty one in the outdated kit.

THERAPIST: Hmmm. Maybe dig that old racket out then and practise a few serves in the back garden. Feeling the racket in your hand will start to activate some muscle memory. And check out what they're wearing on Thursday. If they're dripping in designer-tech let's bin that idea and find something else.

CLIENT: Really?

THERAPIST: It's meant to be fun, remember. So what's our timeline? What can you do today?

CLIENT: Find the racket... tomorrow and Wednesday maybe whack a few shuttles...

THERAPIST: And...

CLIENT: Snoop around on Thursday. If it looks crap, let's dump it.

The therapist puts much more meat on the bones of the plan, thinking up a few of the challenges involved. We all tend to have dialectical swings in our motivation; *I'll do it – no I won't – yes I will*. The dialogue makes that process more overt. The therapist predicts challenges, helps solve them, presents more, and all the time validates that these are legitimate worries. The do it/ don't do it dialectic is not resolved, because more information is needed. The therapist uses a lot of 'devil's advocate' *This club might not suit you, they might all be pensioners or 16 year olds, if they're wearing designer tech let's bin it*. These are much more effective at generating action than encouragement because they are a closer match to the client's own worries. Despite all this doom-mongering the therapist has elicited a commitment to three things by the end of the exchange, successfully working the dialectic. Even if the client does not follow through on the plan, during this conversation they have mentally engaged with going to the club. The neural architecture underpinning the action has begun to form. When we imagine doing an activity we are more likely to carry it out, which is why behavioural rehearsal is so effective.

I cannot stress enough how important it is to identify the 'life worth living' goals for each client. If they come into session three or four times with near identical chain analyses leading up to a harmful behaviour, it is worth checking if there is a big problem that is being ignored. If the client can't identify goals, start with the basics; somewhere to live, someone to love, something to do.

Unsolvable problems

What if the client was a prominent sportsperson, then had a car accident and could no longer perform? Or if their children have disowned them? Or if they wanted to work as a carer but now have a criminal record? The client feels a terrible loss, and others avoid the topic because there are no solutions. People who have suffered a bereavement say that there comes a time when no one refers to it any more, even though for them it is still huge. If the client has told you of a relentless, painful issue for them, my top tip is to be pro-active with your validation the next time you see them:

> During the week I have been thinking about your situation, and how hard (this problem) is for you to bear.

Getting in first with their key issue is immensely powerful. They will be really surprised that you held onto the information while you were apart, and that you were moved enough to mention it without them having to remind you. It is concrete evidence that they are not alone with their pain. As the weeks go by show periodically that you have not forgotten, that you know they are not starting from a level playing field with everyone else. Things are harder, because they have this problem that pains them and it cannot be solved. When I suggest this pro-active validation sometimes therapists remark, 'But whenever they bring it up I DO validate it, every time'. That's like saying, "I don't know why my partner thinks I don't love them, every time they say they love me, I answer, 'and I love you too'". Only when you have voluntarily touched their pain, raising the topic yourself without them having to thrust it before your eyes, have you earned the right to offer an acceptance strategy.

PART

B

Regulating specific emotions

All emotions are regulated differently, there is no one-size-fits-all.

In the next section the main emotions families are taken one by one and for each emotion the following information is given:

1) When the emotion fits the facts

2) The action urge of the emotion

3) The function of the emotion

4) The signature features

5) An example scenario from a therapy session showing how the therapist rehearses the skills

6) A list of special considerations for regulating the emotion

7) Examples of when the emotion requires up-regulating.

CHAPTER

6

Sadness

When does sadness fit the facts?

Sadness fits the facts when there is a loss. This may be loss of something the person had, or loss of something they anticipated having. For example, if we expect a promotion and don't get it this can be experienced as loss.

In the sadness family: Disappointment, grief, despair, depression, rejection, let down, left out, abandoned, lonely.

Action urges: There are two phases to sadness: The first is to withdraw, and the second is actively seeking what has been lost. This might involve rekindling reminders of it or seeking out something similar to replace it.

Function of the emotion: Nature's first priority is to inhibit further losses, making sure we conserve the resources we have. In this context withdrawing makes complete sense. The second function is to elicit help from others and set about finding or replacing what has been lost.

Signature features of sadness

- **Temperature:** Cool
- **Facial expression:** Downcast eyes, tearfulness, mouth turned down, flaccid lower lip, brow lowered
- **Breathing:** Sobbing, sighing, stilted in-breaths and long out breaths
- **Muscle tone:** Floppy, limbs hanging rather than held firmly
- **Voice tone:** When chronic, slow, low quiet tones. When acute, sobs, cries, whines, wails
- **Posture:** Drooping, hunched, downward looking
- **Gesture:** Shrugging, hand wringing, hand on brows
- **Overt actions:** Seeking isolation, not answering the phone, not eating, pining for the lost item, situation, or person. Fixating on reminders such as photos, music, or familiar places. Going over the events of the loss again and again.

Sadness example scenario

In the following example the client is keen to get back with her ex, but he just wants to be friends. She recently bumped into him in town and they went for coffee. Afterwards she walked home and burned her arm deliberately on a hot iron.

THERAPIST: So you didn't harm yourself until you got home, but when did you first notice the urge? (*T. draws C.'s attention to the context of the emotion.*)

CLIENT: In the café, it was all going really well. We were laughing, like old times. I was thinking, surely he must realise we had something really good together? He wasn't exactly flirting, but you know, he was relaxed and jokey like when we were first together. We'd finished our coffee and he said,

'It's been great to see you'. So I said, 'I really enjoyed it too, we should do it again!' Immediately I just saw this... *look* go across his face. His expression just froze. He kept his voice all cheerful and said, 'We're bound to bump into each other!' Then he got up to leave. I went to hug him and he did hug me back, but I could tell... it was so stiff and awkward. Then he was gone.

THERAPIST: Oh no, just when you thought things were going well... *(T. validates the disappointment).* Was it after the hug that you first had the urge to burn yourself? *(T. aims to pinpoint the timing of the urge.)*

CLIENT: No, at first I was angry, I thought, so you've totally led me on for the last hour? And I felt ok, actually. But on the walk home the anger went, and I just thought, he doesn't want me *(becomes tearful).*

THERAPIST: It must have been such a disappointment, I know how much he meant to you. Anyone would have been hurt at such a rapid change. *(pauses). (T. Does little to interfere here, other than to validate the emotion, as the client has named the emotion and is acting appropriately.)*

CLIENT: It was awful. I got in and went straight to heat up the iron.

THERAPIST: It sounds like burning yourself was at least partly to get away from the emotion, I'm guessing it was an over-whelming sadness? *(T. hypotheses that the self-harm and emotional experience were linked.)*

CLIENT: It was unbearable. I just thought, if I start crying I'll never stop.

THERAPIST: A lot of people have that fear, and sadness is a very painful emotion. No wonder we want to avoid it. And yet if sadness fits the facts, we can run but we can't hide. To get past this emotion in a healthy way we have to work out the amount of the loss, to see if our sadness is about right. Now the main thing here is to stay with what you have lost IN THAT MOMENT, when you were walking home?

(T. highlights the dialectic, we don't like the emotion and yet it is normal. Also teaches the client to assess the context of the emotion.)

CLIENT: I suppose I hadn't lost anything, not really. I was no worse off after our coffee together than I was before.

THERAPIST: Ah, now see how quickly you moved to invalidating your emotion? Yet there WAS a very clear loss. What had you hoped to get from your ex, and ended up walking home without having achieved? *(T. highlights the client's self-invalidation, and coaches how to establish the reality of the loss. Many clients are dismissive of justified sadness.)*

CLIENT: I wanted him to see me as a potential girlfriend again. I know it wasn't exactly a date, but I thought it might lead to one...

THERAPIST: That's right. These are genuine losses. I'm wondering, did you comfort yourself because of these losses? Were you tearful at the time? Did you get any help from others? *(T. coaches the client to accept the loss and assesses for any current skills to manage sadness appropriately.)*

CLIENT: No, I just wanted to get in the house and get the iron. I didn't cry at all. I wanted to feel something else, *anything* else.

THERAPIST: Were you doing anything to actively inhibit sadness? *(T. assesses the client's behavioural responses to sadness.)*

CLIENT: Like what?

THERAPIST: Common actions are tensing your body, clenching your jaw, holding your breath... these are in fact opposite actions to sadness.

CLIENT: I was doing all of those, so why didn't the sadness go down?

THERAPIST: Because the emotion *did* fit the facts, so before we use any methods to feel *less* sad, we have to give voice to the bit that is entirely justified by the facts. This is what we mean by dialectical – that some of the sadness was too much, but some was really valid. We need something you can say to yourself that sums up what you had genuinely lost.

CLIENT: I'd lost everything! Any hope of a future with him, or anyone really – who would I find who is like him? We share so many memories, I was hoping we would get back together, have Christmases like we used to, go to gigs, go on that camper-van tour of France. That's all gone.

THERAPIST: Whoa! This is an example of the pendulum swinging the other way – going from not wanting to feel any sadness at all, to feeling way too much. When sadness starts up it really runs away with you. Is that what happened on that day, as you walked home? *(T. highlights more how sadness quickly escalates.)*

CLIENT: It felt bigger and bigger until I thought I would burst.

THERAPIST: OK, so we might start with the skill of mindful describing, which is kind of validating yourself, that you have every right to feel sad. Say something about what made you sad, in that moment, but pare it down to the things that you'd lost on that day. Have a go. *(T. outlines the skill of mindful describing and encourages behavioural rehearsal.)*

CLIENT: 'I wanted to meet up again, but he didn't'.

THERAPIST: Now I want you to run this through your wise mind and see if it *feels* right, it has to really touch the truth of what you were sad about. *(T. does not assume this is accurate but asks the client to assess. This is strengthening C.'s sense of self.)*

CLIENT: No, it doesn't, there's something missing. That wasn't the worst thing…

THERAPIST: Great observing. So add the worst bit in. 'I'm sad because…' *(T. encourages C. to evaluate the accuracy for herself and to improve it.)*

CLIENT: I'm sad because I really thought we had a chance *(looks pained)* and then his hug was so cold.

THERAPIST: That second attempt seems to get more of your dashed hopes into it. Only *you* know what was going on inside you, so you need to check it out, is that what was making you sad? *(T. gives the message that it is C. who has the final say on her internal experience, and also this is acting as exposure to the sadness cue, allowing her to experience it without fear.)*

CLIENT: I just thought we could be back as a couple, with all the things that go with it. I wanted him to *want* me. And I knew that he didn't, well, he didn't show it. *(Client becomes tearful.)*

THERAPIST: That was very mindful – and it IS sad, there's no shame in wanting that closeness, the songbooks are full of anthems to unrequited love... films, poetry, everyone recognises this type of sadness. Just let the tears come... That's great. *(T. normalises sadness in this context and waits for the wave of sadness to subside. T. keeps a matter of fact tone, not overly sympathetic, so as not to flood the client with more cues to sadness. The aim is to allow behavioural rehearsal of experiencing the emotion.)*

CLIENT: *(Crying)* I always think it's just me, that everyone else is happily coupled up. So I try really hard not to cry, in case I never stop. If I burn myself it stops me wanting to cry, it's like I go into shock instead...

THERAPIST: Most people will not cry for any more than seven minutes in one go, unless they keep reminding themselves of the sadness over and over again. That's why we need to make sure we stick to the facts. *(T. gives psychoeducation on emotion.)* If you are scared of crying we need to practise you crying some proper 'ploppy'* tears without blocking them. Remember you said you were holding your breath

---

* 'Ploppy' tears are those that roll down the cheeks and plop onto your book or your knee. Clients appreciate the descriptive term, as it normalises the thing they fear the most.

and clenching your jaw, as well as tensing your muscles. So right now, here with me, just try relaxing into the sadness. Say something about the sadness again, and allow your breath to come in long sighs. *(T. encourages behavioural rehearsal of accepting the emotion.)*

CLIENT: I thought we had a chance to be closer, but he didn't want that, and it showed in his hug.

THERAPIST: Did you tense up there? I just noticed your jaw? What happened? *(T. is awake to signs that the client is inhibiting sadness.)*

CLIENT: Yes, I was just thinking about the future

THERAPIST: Remember your mindfulness, bring your mind back to relaxing your muscles, and letting the tears flow. You won't cry forever, I promise. There's a difference between crying *willing* tears, that allow the grief to pass, and trying to squash your tears down so they have to squeeze out like water oozing through the cracks in a dam. *(T. offers a metaphor.)* How does that feel? *(T. checks the behavioural effects of the intervention.)*

CLIENT: Not as bad as I thought, but I'm scared when I'm on my own that this will just get out of control.

THERAPIST: OK, I am going to let you into a secret, but you have to use this information really wisely. If the sadness gets TOO big then you can deliberately tense your muscles, stand up straight, put a firm tone in your voice, hold your breath a little, just as you were doing before. It will reduce the intensity. It will work better than when you did it before, on the walk home, because at the same time you're acknowledging why you are sad – the validating bit. It's both/and, not just trying to escape, but showing you understand the message from the sadness. Now, personally, I don't recommend you do this until you have cried for a full seven minutes, to take the edge off the buildup. You CAN tolerate that, and then down-regulating will be easier. You will have a bit more confidence to let yourself be sad, if you know how to stop it when it overwhelms you. Try it now. *(T gets the client to do a behavioural rehearsal of opposite action to sadness.)*

CLIENT: *(Adopts a more upright posture, uses a firm voice tone.)* 'I'm sad because I thought we could be back as a couple, with all the things that go with it. I wanted him to want to meet up again, but he left without doing that'.

THERAPIST: Did you feel how you can get either more sadness or less sadness by tweaking those domains – your face, your posture, your voice, your breathing, your muscles, etc.? You did well. Another 'opposite action' is seeking out company rather than isolating yourself. Is there anyone you could invite round? *(T. reinforces goal-relevant behaviour and teaches how to take the edge off the sadness through opposite action.)*

CLIENT: Maybe Darius.

THERAPIST: OK. Remember – if you are a bit phobic of sadness and just go straight to opposite action, without doing those emotion validations *it will not work*. That's going back to building a dam, and eventually it will overflow. So check that it actually *feels* sad enough. That might sound odd, because who really wants to be sad? But if the amount of sadness you feel is too low to fit the facts, you are just storing it up for later. On the other hand, if you are tipping into tragic sadness when the facts don't justify that, then do some opposite action, firm up your muscles, even hold your breath for a few seconds. We are neither trying to dismiss the emotion or ramp it up, just to get it in perspective for that one moment. *(T. Reminds the client of dialectical theory.)*

CLIENT: But why can't I just get rid of it completely? Like when I burn myself?

THERAPIST: Because the emotion is telling you something important, dismiss or deny that and it will come back stronger next time. And that brings us to our next question. Can we resolve the sadness at its source, which is either to get your ex back in your life, or find a replacement for what you had with him? *(T. gives psychoeducation on emotion.)*

CLIENT: I don't think he is going to come back. But I am scared of making new relationships.

THERAPIST: It's all related – if you can't handle sadness, then you won't want to make new partnerships, because loving always involves some loss. So while you are in therapy we need to start building your plans to counter loneliness. We can make a list of actions like joining clubs, volunteering, dating apps. You might not be ready right now, but we can lay out the path for when you are. If we don't, you will always be left longing for the return of your ex. *(T. describes how one set of problems impact on other things. This is also dialectical theory.)*

CLIENT: Erm. when you put it like that… well ok, there's no harm in making a list.

THERAPIST: Good. So let's recap our Emotion regulation for today:

- You identified the sadness and described it mindfully.
- You validated your right to feel it.
- You pared it down to the loss you felt TODAY.
- You allowed yourself to cry freely for that loss.
- You knew how to act opposite if the emotion was running away with you.
- You have some long-term plans to reduce loneliness.

Now do you think if you had done this when you left the café you would have been more likely or less likely to burn yourself? *(T summarises the set of emotion regulation skills and checks the effect on the target behaviour.)*

CLIENT: I think if I had just known that there was something I could do about the sadness it would have helped enormously. I thought it would go on until something in me broke.

THERAPIST: Allowing appropriate sadness without fear will take practice. When you are not with me the emotion will feel more raw, and acting this way will be harder, so every time you feel a little sadness, do your practice, and if you need any help let me know. Now, let's get back to that list. *(T. refocusses on problem-solving.)*

Special considerations in regulating sadness

1) In sadness the therapist's use of down-regulation should be sparing. More often than not the client is trying to get rid of the emotion, and needs coaching in how to tolerate it. The development of self-validation, and the ability to sit with justified sadness is important.

2) Clients may use medication, substances, keeping busy and oversleeping to down-regulate sadness, which tends to compound loss, creating a vicious cycle.

3) Nature allows us to delay grief. For example, if you are a soldier and your colleague is killed in battle, you are able to continue fighting and then grieve at the point of reaching safety. Unfortunately this pause-facility means clients can build up a backlog, so each new sadness sets off memories of associated losses. Learning to do sadness mindfully (what has been lost in *this* moment) is crucial.

4) As in the example above, anger can be preferable to sadness (while the client was angry with her ex, she did not feel like burning herself) When the anger is no longer present the sadness takes its place.

5) Asking a client to repeatedly describe the cue (e.g. 'I was sad he didn't want to meet up') is a form of exposure, so the emotion may go up briefly before coming down.

6) Sadness from one event, such as losing your job, can vary throughout the day. For example, at 8:00 am your sadness may be high as you have no job to go to. At 7pm when you are at home with your family you are not suffering such a loss in that moment. If friends call round and are talking about what they did at work that day, your loss may creep up again. This is also true of bereavement; Clients sometimes say after a death, 'I felt really guilty that I was laughing at the funeral, but we were all together and reminiscing'. This is because the sadness comes and goes according to the situation, and that's as it should be.

7) Adopting a soothing or sympathetic tone with the client can be experienced by them as 'flooding' (which is why they sometimes say, 'Don't be nice to me I will start crying'.) It is better to adopt a matter-of-fact tone at the beginning, and increase the intensity of your sympathy strategically – i.e. within the principles of shaping the client to tolerate increasingly more intense cues.

8) If the client says what they are sad about, believe them. It can be unhelpful to contradict them or offer alternatives, even if it seems obvious to you that they were really sad about some other thing. Instead, regulate around whatever they have identified. Does it fit the facts? If not, do opposite action. If the sadness doesn't reduce, ask, 'Is it possible there was something else making you sad in that moment?' This helps *the client* negotiate the convoluted path of their emotional experiences.

9) If the client is very emotion phobic choose carefully which links in the chain to work on. Start on smaller losses, rather than the most poignant ones. Remember the question, 'So what had you lost *in that moment?*'

10) Incremental differences in levels of sadness can be hard to grasp. One supervisee was dealing with a girl frequently

crippled by overwhelming sadness. The client had mild learning difficulties and only learnt one level of distinction; that big losses were 'tragically sad'. She learnt to say, 'I was sad, but not *tragically* sad' and even that made a huge difference. Words like 'disappointed', 'sorry', and 'hurt' can show lower level emotion, whilst 'gutted', 'devastated', 'heartbroken' represent higher levels.

11) Signs that clients are blocking sadness are: Holding their breath, excessive swallowing, pressing lips together tightly or blinking away tears. If this happens instruct the client (using a neutral tone) to breathe instead of swallowing, etc.

12) It's helpful to distinguish 'willing tears' – those the client allows, from 'breakthrough tears' which are those that simply breach all the client's defences and tumble out despite their best inhibitory efforts. (I have been known to sponsor a client for every minute of 'willing tears' that they were able to cry. The money went to a charity of their choice.)

13) It is natural for families or carers to want to soothe, and they can become biased towards distraction; *'Don't think about it, you're better off without him. Here, play your music, or shall we go shopping?'* Well-meaning but invalidating (unless now is just not the right time to be sad. For example, a friend going through a divorce described her gratitude that a colleague noticed she was on the verge of tears walking to a meeting, and distracted her so she could get through. 'It depends', right?).

14) If the client cycles rapidly between anxiety and sadness many therapists will opt to work on reducing the anxiety. However, in my experience if the client can handle sadness better they often become less anxious.

15) If the client flees into another emotion like anger you may need to highlight and block that by returning to the cue for sadness. Michaela Swales and I have produced a video of exposure to a cue that elicits sadness, with subtitles

describing the therapist's strategies, available from British Isles DBT training, info@dbt-training.co.uk

16) Long-term avoidance plays havoc with the way emotions are presented. Working with a client with alcohol problems it took a while to realise that the shaking and sweating were not always anxiety, but efforts to control sadness.

When does sadness need up-regulating?

If the client encounters a cue that would normally set off sadness, but shows no signs of it, then you might want to draw their attention to when the emotion would be appropriate, and where they might feel it in their body. I have given an example scenario in Chapter 4. Linehan says that clients sometimes respond to sadness by saying, 'I don't care', and she follows that with the question, 'Is it that you don't care, or that you don't allow yourself to care?' An example might be care-leavers having to vacate placements because they reach the age where the finance is no longer available. Shrugging and saying 'I'm not bothered' could be highly functional in the short term to get them through the move. The therapist would perhaps highlight the pros and cons of such protective distancing.

I have also seen in supervision therapists pursue an agenda of 'getting the client to cry' when they are not ready, by which I mean when it is not an item that has cropped up in the chain, and there is no 'invitation to treat':

THERAPIST: I'm glad I brought up the issue of your Nan today, I could tell you really needed to cry about that loss, you have bottled this up for such a long time, well done for getting in touch with that feeling.

CLIENT: *(in floods of tears)* Yes, I miss her so much, thank you for understanding. *(Never returns to therapy again.)*

CHAPTER 7   Anger

When does anger fit the facts?

Anger fits the facts when you are blocked in pursuit of a goal or threatened.

In the anger family: Rage, fury, crossness, annoyance, irritation, frustration, wound up, aggression.

Action urges: To attack.

Function of the emotion: To give you an energy boost to either burst through the obstacle or repel the threat.

Signature features of anger

- **Temperature:** Hot
- **Facial expression:** Frowning, glaring, pursing the lips, glowering, snarling, clenched jaw
- **Breathing:** Fast, shallow
- **Muscle tone:** Tense
- **Voice tone:** Raised volume, firm

- **Posture:** Head or chin jutting forwards, squared up to the target of the anger, clenched fists, shoulders raised, hands on hips
- **Gesture:** Finger-jabbing, fist-shaking, kicking
- **Overt actions:** Slamming doors, storming or barging around, following the target of the anger, sullen silences, sulking.

Anger example scenario

In the following example the client was at home with her husband when her 28-year-old stepdaughter arrived at the house asking for money. An argument ensued after which the client had urges to overdose.

THERAPIST: At what point did you notice the urge to overdose?
(T. establishes the context for the emotion.)

CLIENT: Ivan just contradicted everything I said to Suzy. I told her we didn't have any spare money, and he was saying things like, 'Now wait a minute, we could look at what we've got...' Does he think I'm lying? He doesn't know our outgoings. And even if we had any spare, he should back me up. We should have those discussions in private not in front of Suzy. She rocks up and he just wants to give in to her.

THERAPIST: So as soon as you heard the contradiction, you had the urge to harm yourself? Was that during the argument?
(T. seeks further clarification on timing, so as to assess the controlling variables.)

CLIENT: No, it was after Suzy had gone, and I asked Ivan why he hadn't backed me up. He said, 'lets talk about it when you're calmer'. That is SO annoying, because it means if I raise my voice I am proving I am *not calm*. Then he went into the kitchen and I was fuming. I could hear him whistling a little tune and I know for a fact if I had walked in there he would have been cleaning the counter tops even though they are perfectly clean because I ALREADY CLEANED THEM. I really wanted to go in there and wrap that wet cloth around his face. But you know what would happen if I did that? He would just have the upper hand, and I would be the one who was 'disturbed', that's what he calls me. Every fibre in my body was tense, I went upstairs and just thought, I'm exhausted, I just want to go to sleep and not wake up.

THERAPIST: The urge to overdose was to escape the tension? *(T. establishes the function of the target behaviour.)* And I think you are hinting at the name of the emotion… *(T. pulls for the skill of labelling emotion).*

CLIENT: Escape or scream the place down. It was definitely anger

THERAPIST: Really intense anger? *(T. encourages the client to rate the emotion's intensity.)*

CLIENT: It was off the scale.

THERAPIST: Well in a moment we can look at how you managed to resist the urge, but for now I just want to focus on that anger. I mentioned escape, but maybe the urge to overdose was just to reduce it? *(T. links emotion regulation to the target behaviour.)*

CLIENT: The thing is, I DO reduce my anger, like Ivan says, 'just get over it', or 'count to ten' and all that. I sleep it off, or drink it away. The next day things were back to normal, for him anyway. So getting my anger down is not the problem.

THERAPIST: I agree. You use a number of strategies to put the anger behind you, to some extent, anyway. But now we need to do proper emotion regulation, and not just distract you from the thing that made you angry. A degree of anger was justified, it's telling you something important. *(T. discourages just distracting away from the emotion.)*

CLIENT: I think that too, it IS justified, but Ivan says I'm over reacting.

THERAPIST: Then let's work out how much of the emotion fitted the facts that day, so we have a rough idea of the level of anger we want to keep. Can you remember from group when Anger fits the facts? *(T. elicits one element of the skill 'check the facts' which is understanding when the emotion is justified.)*

CLIENT: When you are threatened?

THERAPIST: That's part of it, and the other part? *(T. shapes the skill.)*

CLIENT: I don't know.

THERAPIST: When you are blocked in pursuit of a goal. So first we need to work out which goals were being blocked that evening. *(T. teaches orients the client to the function of the emotion.)*

CLIENT: I didn't have any goals. It was Suzy trying to get money from us, and Ivan not sticking up for me.

THERAPIST: That might have made you vulnerable, but during the argument you didn't have the urge to harm yourself. I'm thinking more about when your anger was peaking, when Ivan was in the kitchen. What was it you were trying to get from Ivan and failing? *(T. helps the client check out what she felt she was being blocked from doing.)*

CLIENT: I wanted him to see my side of it. And for him to apologise for not sticking up for me, and to stop pretending to clean, and to have a proper argument without running away and blaming me.

THERAPIST: Quite a lot of goals there, I'd say: You wanted some validation, Ivan to hear you out, and an apology. And you didn't get those things? *(T. walks the client through the behaviour of identifying blocked goals.)*

CLIENT: Fat chance of any of those.

THERAPIST: I think you are probably right, and in that moment, you did one of the strategies that reduces anger, in that you walked away from the provocation. That was better than hitting him with a wet cloth. But it sounds like once you had walked away you kind of dropped your goals, leaving you with this awful frustration? *(T. reinforces opposite action of walking away rather than lashing out, and affirms that the client's goals were **still** important.)*

CLIENT: That's right.

THERAPIST: OK, so let's take the goal of validation. It is perfectly reasonable to want validation from Ivan, and it's also reasonable to decide *in that moment* you were not likely to get it. Both of you were angry. So now we need to just keep hold of that valid part of the emotion, and not let it go. This is dialectics in action, both things are true – that you are unlikely to get it in this moment AND that it is still valid to want it. I wonder did you engage in any self-validation when you went upstairs? *(T. coaches dialectics, moving away from an all-or-nothing position.)*

CLIENT: No, I was just thinking he should be giving it to me

THERAPIST: And there is some truth in that, we all like support from a partner. Doing some self-validation won't stop Ivan giving you validation of he's up for it. These are not either/or, it can be both/and. One problem is that our thought processes are pretty much wiped out by strong emotion. So bearing in mind that this is definitely NOT about letting Ivan off the hook – we are going to deal with him later – are you willing to try some physiological strategies, just to give us some thinking space? *(T. seeks an invitation to treat, and continually validates the emotion.)*

CLIENT: OK, how would it work?

THERAPIST: Well, first it is hard to be furious if you lie flat, so you might have laid down on the bed, or just stretch your body back in the chair – it's why we use the expression, 'being laid-back'. Also if you smooth out any frown lines on your forehead and drop your shoulders down, that will help lower the 'anger' signals going from your body back to your brain. Try now just leaning back in your seat and smoothing your hand over your face. *(T. encourages the client to behaviourally rehearse opposite action in the domains of posture and facial expression.)*

CLIENT: No, that's stupid.

THERAPIST: Hmm... do you know what triggered that thought? Was it to do with how you'll appear here to me, or something to do with not reducing the anger towards Ivan? *(T. assesses for controlling variables of the therapy-interfering behaviour.)*

CLIENT: *(Shrugs)*

THERAPIST: I was once about to serve a meringue at a dinner party and accidently burnt my hand taking it out of the oven. What do you think I should do first, serve the guests or run my arm under the cold tap? *(T. uses a metaphor to demonstrate the importance of attending to physiology. Telling a personal story also takes some focus off the client, which may diffuse the tension.)*

CLIENT: See to the burn

THERAPIST: Agreed, and your fight with Ivan 'burnt' your feelings, so we are going to reduce the heat before taking on the rest of the argument. I'd like you to have some confidence that it can work, that's why I am suggesting we try it. But I won't be rigid (shrugs), I'll be guided by you. *(T. models flexibility, demonstrating being dialectical. Even if the client does not comply, the teaching points have not been completely lost. T. Also highlights the client's freedom to choose.)*

CLIENT: *(Sighs)* OK, what do I do?

THERAPIST: The sighing is great start, because elongating the breath is an opposite action for anger. So breathe out, sit back, and let your shoulders drop, then smooth out your forehead, with your fingers if necessary. If your jaw is clenched then loosen it. Yes, that's great. Has the tension you just felt with me gone up, gone down or stayed the same? *(T. elicits behavioural rehearsal and encourage the client to evaluate the outcome.)*

CLIENT: *(Breathing out in long exhalations)* er... it's lower...

THERAPIST: OK, anger is a hot emotion so it helps if you can cool yourself down, too. What could you have done to reduce your temperature? *(T. pulls for more behaviour from the client, identifying opposite actions.)*

CLIENT: I have a fan in my bedroom, so I can put that on... I could have got a cold drink

THERAPIST: Great. Now we don't want to get the anger all the way to zero, we want to remove the bit that's over the top. I think this is where you have been going wrong in the past. If you just try and leave the anger behind it feels like there was a fight and you lost. We want to keep your goals in mind and revisit them when you're not as furious. From now on remind yourself, 'I'm getting my anger down but ONLY so I can get my point across'. Try saying that. *(T. elicits the behaviour so the client can feel the difference.)*

CLIENT: *(Complies)* That sounds good.

THERAPIST: OK, so how much crossness would have roughly fitted the facts? Where 100% is the most anger you could possibly feel *(T. reminds the client to check the facts, and encourages her to have a go.)*

CLIENT: 100% because He ALWAYS does this.

THERAPIST: OK, so we need to use mindfulness – it's about *this* moment. Bringing in past events will pump the anger up.

CLIENT: ...And I was LIVID.

THERAPIST: For sure, but if we only ever have anger as FULL ON or OFF, you have nowhere to go if he does something worse. How angry would you need to be if say, he told you he had re-mortgaged the house and gambled the lot away? Or posted naked pictures of you on the internet? We can't have those things at the same level as for an argument where he didn't back you up. *(T. explains the dialectical skill of discernment, assessing an appropriate level for the emotion.)*

CLIENT: When you put it like that, ok, maybe I'd want to be at 30%.

THERAPIST: Fine, so we can stop down-regulating when you feel it's about right, it's not an exact science, you will get to feel different levels eventually. Just remember to keep some crossness but not outright rage. Imagine yourself back there in your bedroom and talk me through what you're doing. *(T. Coaches flexibility in learning the skill and elicits more rehearsal.)*

CLIENT: *(Complies with the instructions)* OK, so now I don't feel as angry, but I'm still cross, so then what?

THERAPIST: Good, now validate yourself by saying something that fits the facts, such as, 'I was telling the truth about what we could afford and I expected him to back me up' but instead of saying it with a livid tone of voice and furious facial expression, tone down the reaction a little. *(T. Coaches self-validation, with some opposite action.)*

CLIENT: *(Complies)* Hmm... I see what you mean, about making myself feel better. But I can say it all I like, he still disagrees.

THERAPIST: Right, and because you are worried about being branded as 'kicking off' you kind of lose the truth in your own side. *(T. clarifies the consequences of always seeking external validation.)* And what you say to yourself during this bit also helps with what you are going to say to Ivan. The secret is to wait until you can say it calmly, without insisting on a response. *(T. links down-regulating excess anger with being effective in communicating crossness to Ivan – thereby validating the client's goal.)*

CLIENT: What? No response! But what about my apology?

THERAPIST: If you can't *guarantee* getting something, it is better to describe it as a preference rather than a goal. For example, I'd prefer if Ivan apologised *(T. models how to moderate goals)* and let me ask you an interesting question, when Ivan had *his* say and went into the kitchen, was he expecting a response from you?

CLIENT: No, it's like once he'd finished talking, that was that.

THERAPIST: So imagine that it's completely calm between the two of you, and you say, 'I know the yesterday you wanted us to give the money to Suzy, and at the same time I was telling the truth when I said we couldn't afford it'. And then YOU are the one who goes into the kitchen and does that cleaning thing. Not in a sulky way, but just showing that once you'd had your say, the matter was closed. There's a degree of self-validation right there. *(T. models how to represent your case without needing a response.)*

CLIENT: That would feel great!

THERAPIST: OK, but you might have noticed I added in a little dialectics there – because I said, 'I know you wanted to give the money to Suzy AND AT THE SAME TIME I was telling the truth'. This is giving some validation to Ivan as well as to yourself. Remember our fast skills. If you acknowledge the other person's side, you can't be accused of overreacting. So It's hard for him to come back at you in a hostile way. It also helps to get your voice more reasonable if you can be a bit kind. So let's imagine it's the next day and you are both sitting on the sofa, here, use this chair and I'll pretend to be Ivan watching TV. Now show me how you'll do it. *(T. elicits behavioural rehearsal.)*

CLIENT: 'Ivan, I know you wanted to give Suzy money, and at the same time, I was telling the truth when I said we can't afford it'. *(Gets up and walks away.)*

THERAPIST: Not bad, though you did a bit of a strut there at the end, is that the amount of anger you wanted to portray? *(T. Gives feedback, and engages the client in evaluating the skill.)*

CLIENT: Yes, I wanted to do that.

THERAPIST: Then that's fine, it wasn't over the top for the situation. You can do more of your interpersonal skills and ask for an apology if you wish, but that would, maybe, give Ivan more control of the situation than you want him to have. *(T. does not try and tone down the response, the final say is with the client.)*

CLIENT: No, I like the idea of walking away, and I don't feel guilty, because I did validate him, too.

THERAPIST: You did! Well done! So let's recap; when you had gone upstairs on that day, if you had known how to take the edge off the anger through opposite action, if you had done some self-validation, and had some confidence that you could communicate your crossness to Ivan without a row, would you have been more likely to want to overdose, or less likely? *(T. assesses for the impact of the skill on the target behaviour.)*

CLIENT: I think I'd have felt better, so less likely!

THERAPIST: Great, so we've done lots of change strategies, and DBT is all about acceptance and change, so what things do we have to accept? *(T. pulls for evidence of an acceptance skill.)*

CLIENT: That I can't *make* Ivan apologise.

THERAPIST: Right, or even make him see it your way, but you CAN have your say, which was one of the goals that the anger was bringing to your attention. *(T. reminds the client of the function of the emotion.)*

Special considerations in regulating anger

1) One of the best interventions I ever learnt in DBT was to say to the client, 'How much anger do we want to keep in this situation?' And to say it *before* addressing the excess emotion. This phrase is so unexpected and so validating that

there is instant buy-in from the client. After working on their legitimate anger (and there is usually at least some) they are much more willing to collaborate on down-regulating to the required amount. People who have lost control often feel ashamed or judged, and find it a relief to hear, 'Actually it is ok to be cross and I can help you express that'. It takes down the tension in the body that is needed to open the client up to new ways of responding.

2) Clients will often agree that anger is excessive when it results in harm or the urge to attack. Avoid getting embroiled in an argument about it, stay neutral in tone, and point out that as a good rule of thumb, we're anti-harm.

3) Anger is often a secondary emotion, as people prefer it to a feeling of sadness or shame. In the scenario above, if the primary emotion had been sadness, then as the anger went down the sadness would have bubbled up.

4) When clients are not motivated to down-regulate anger it might be because they feel they are losing face. This is why it is imperative to focus on the valid part of the anger first.

5) Coaching clients to see things from the other person's point of view and be kind is part of 'opposite action'. I think of it as the advanced component of this skill. In the scenario above if the client was amenable she might have put herself in Ivan's shoes, perhaps by mindfully describing, 'Ivan wants Suzy to see him as a good father'. Timing is crucial, too early and you invalidate the client's position.

6) There is a myth that if someone is angry with an absent person, they can 'get the anger out' by punching a cushion, or hitting a punchbag. On the whole, acting violently only increases physiological arousal.

7) Judgements tend to push up anger, and can be made verbally – e.g. 'he never listens to me'. They can also be implied through tone of voice or a facial expression.

For example, saying, 'He was in the kitchen cleaning' can be changed completely by stressing the word CLEANING and adding an eye-roll, or tutting.

8) It is harder for the therapist when the anger seems irrational. For example, two clients are allocated support workers in the same week, and one is furious that the other received the same level of service. It does not appear that this is either threatening or blocking. But the client may feel this blocks them from being taken as seriously.

9) Some clients appear angry when anxious. Assess, don't assume.

10) Victims of violence may become phobic of anger in others or themselves. These are the clients who might benefit from being shown you can frown, or make a cross face, or have a cross tone in your voice and no bad things happen.

11) Therapists working in prisons describe how certain over-controlled personality types have a characteristic pattern before an assault, sometimes referred to as 'brooding' anger. The client goes silent and still. This may be accompanied by 'squaring up to' the intended victim by making the body posture larger.

12) There is no substitute for knowing your patient, and it's worth asking, 'What should I look out for to tell me you are angry?'

When does anger need up-regulating?

Some clients have had very bad experiences in the past when either they or someone else in their environment got angry. Clients with BPD are sensitive to much lower levels of anger (Veague and Hooley 2014). The emotion needs up-regulating where a degree of anger would be appropriate and functional, but is absent.

I am not routinely including up-regulation scenarios in this book, but include a brief example for anger as it often trips therapists up. In this snippet a client's teenage sons have thrown eggs at the neighbours' windows, eliciting multiple complaints. She feels pressure to control them, but has always been afraid to show anger.

THERAPIST: I know you didn't actually feel angry with them, rather you felt that your neighbours were judging you, and you wished the boys were better behaved. Would it have been helpful though, for the boys to get the message that you were cross about this? *(T. gives a rationale for up-regulating anger.)*

CLIENT: I think so, but I really don't do anger.

THERAPIST: Sure, it's just that you might want to expand your repertoire. It's up to you, but if you had wanted to show some crossness, what level would have been about right? *(T. Coaches how to check the facts.)*

CLIENT: Er. maybe two out of ten.

THERAPIST: OK, you can add in a few subtle signature features, till you are just showing crossness at two out of ten. You probably won't feel cross, but that's ok. So what about trying a cross tone of voice, it's a good place to start. *(T. coaches elements of up-regulating, focussing on a relatively easy domain to change.)* Try saying 'That was NOT how I expect you to behave'.

CLIENT: I wouldn't say that, though.

THERAPIST: You can change the words if you like. Or do you mean you just don't tell them if they are at fault?

CLIENT: I would just say, *(sighs)* 'I wish you'd stop annoying the neighbours'.

THERAPIST: Ah, so more like a comment. Those words are fine, if you drop the first bit, and say, 'Stop annoying the neighbours'.

We just need to get your voice firmer and louder, and your posture taller – here, stand up, head a bit higher, chin forward. Try it now with more force in your tone. *(T. reinforces on-target behaviour and gives corrective feedback.)*

CLIENT: (Complies with the instructions.)

THERAPIST: Better! Try frowning a little. That would help. *(T. adds more corrective feedback.)*

CLIENT: *(Complies)* But I don't feel angry inside.

THERAPIST: That's ok, it takes time for your brain to package this all up into something that feels like 'anger'. But even without the sensations inside, you might immediately get some benefits – in that your boys might realise their behaviour is not acceptable. It's hard for them to get that when there is a total lack of crossness. We can try it, and see what happens. *(T. coaches 'fake it till you make it' and draws attention to consequences.)*

Reference

Veague, H. B., & Hooley, J. M. (2014). Enhanced sensitivity and response bias for male anger in women with borderline personality disorder. *Psychiatry Research, 215*(3), 687–693.

CHAPTER

8

Fear and anxiety

When do fear and anxiety fit the facts?

Fear fits the facts when there is danger. Linehan says it is when there is a serious danger to your life, your health, or your well-being. For example, losing your home, your job, or a very significant relationship would count as situations in which fear is justified.

In the fear family: Afraid, frightened, anxious, worried, fretting, nervous, scared, jumpy, fidgety, strung out, terrified, cautious, apprehensive.

Action urges: (Anxiety) Run away, avoid (pure fear) freeze, play dead.

Function of the emotion: To keep us safe from danger by either avoiding it or freezing until the danger (which in evolution was probably a predator) has passed us by.

Signature features of anxiety (stage 1 of fear)

Anxiety is thought to occur when the danger is still far enough away that the person can flee from it.

- **Temperature:** Hot, sweating – getting the muscles primed to run
- **Facial expression:** Red-faced, eyes wide under brows that are pulled inwards towards the centre. Mouth is slightly open (making it easier to breathe rapidly) characteristic lip biting may be to remind us that even though the mouth is open we need to keep silent
- **Breathing:** Rapid and shallow
- **Muscle tone:** Tense
- **Voice tone:** High, sometimes speechless
- **Posture:** Shoulders up, hands clasped, or grip tightened
- **Gesture:** Shaking, Fidgeting, pacing, toes lifting or tapping, twitching, jumpy (like a cat on hot bricks)
- **Overt actions:** Checking behaviours, eyeing exit routes, watchfulness.

Pure fear signature features

These are thought to occur when the danger is so close that the person cannot outrun or escape it:

- **Temperature:** Cold, extremities may be icy to the touch
- **Facial expression:** Pale-faced, Eyes wide, eyebrows high, mouth open
- **Breathing:** Jagged, breath-holding
- **Muscle tone:** Tense
- **Voice tone:** High

- **Posture:** May just be frozen in the immediate posture, but if there is time to move it can result in a tight body-frame, pulled inwards, making the person appear smaller. Cowering, curling up
- **Gesture:** Trembling, hairs may stand out on the arms or back of the neck
- **Overt actions:** Pure fear is characteristically inactive.

Anxiety example scenario

In the following example a client cut himself after worrying about an argument in which his landlord threatened to evict him. The therapist has already worked on getting rid of the blade, and is now going to hone in on the emotion link in the chain.

THERAPIST: So you cut yourself at 11pm, and you were thinking about the incident a few days ago where your landlord said he'd had more complaints from the people upstairs. *(T. summarises the links in the chain.)*

CLIENT: Yes, he said, 'that's the last straw, you are out. You'll be hearing from me'. He was pretty angry. *(Client looks anxious, eyes darting.)*

THERAPIST: It sounds pretty full on *(T. looks appropriately concerned).* Is there a danger that you do have to be out by this time next week? *(T. validates by showing a facial expression of worry, and encourages the client to establish if fear matches the facts.)*

CLIENT: No, he didn't say anything like that. So, it's been, like, four days and I haven't had any letters or anything. He hasn't been back. It's all gone quiet. It's probably OK.

THERAPIST: *(maintains the concerned expression)* I guess you need to know how long the notice period would be? *(T. notices the client has escaped into reassuring himself, so holds the facial cue for anxiety a little longer, whilst asking the client to behaviourally rehearse checking the facts.)*

CLIENT: I pay my rent monthly, but I'm not sure if that was just him being cross or if it was an official notice to quit. It could just have been talking in temper? *(Client is sweating, and his voice is quivering.)* Legally I think he has to put it in writing. But I haven't had anything. It's not knowing. He can't just throw me out, can he? It's their word against mine, they make loads more noise than me.

THERAPIST: Sounds like it's really hanging over you... Thinking back to the teaching we did in group on emotions, which emotion do you think you were having just before you cut yourself? *(T. refers to emotion regulation teaching from group.)*

CLIENT: I was scared. I don't want to be out on the street.

THERAPIST: Anyone would be anxious at the thought of losing their home. Remember there are some subtle differences between types of fear – do you think it was pure fear – that you were cold and felt kind of paralysed, or do you think it was anxiety where you were hot and fidgety? *(T. validates and coaches more detailed identification of the emotion.)*

CLIENT: Anxiety. I was really jumpy.

THERAPIST: Sounds about right, anxiety tends to come when we are worried about a *future* danger. And on a scale of 0–100 how high was it? *(T. coaches the client to identify the level of his emotion.)*

CLIENT: 100.

THERAPIST: So let's work out if that level matches the facts. The threat of losing your home does sound genuine. Can you call the landlord and ask? *(T. suggests active information gathering.)*

CLIENT: But if he is starting to cool down I might set him off again.

THERAPIST: Hmm, you're right. There may be a risk of rekindling his anger, so perhaps it's better not to phone. See how that little bit of anxiety helped us out, there? It stopped us jumping in and making it worse. *(T. highlights that having anxiety about phoning is helpful.)* If we can't find out, we have nothing to lose by making a plan, just in case. So it might be helpful to take the edge off that anxiety first. Do you remember the action urge for anxiety? *(T. links the reduction in anxiety to effective problem-solving and pulls for some emotion regulation, identifying an action urge.)*

CLIENT: Is it avoid? Run away?

THERAPIST: Yes, and there are so many ways of running away. One is using denial, e.g. telling yourself it won't happen. But because there is a genuine threat that it *could* happen, that might not work out too well – what do you think? Are you convincing yourself that there is no threat? *(T. demands active participation from the client, to evaluate whether his strategies are working or not.)*

CLIENT: *(Pauses)* Not really. It feels OK for a while...

THERAPIST: Another is by trying to get rid of the feeling, by cutting yourself. That seemed to work at least in the short term? *(T. clarifies the behavioural consequences of cutting.)*

CLIENT: Yes, but it came back.

THERAPIST: So denial and cutting are not working. That's because trying to avoid the emotion distracts us from solving the problem. We might have ways to avoid homelessness, one is to make sure you have somewhere to go if you are evicted. The other is to negotiate with the landlord to stay on. *(T. explains how shifting focus to avoiding the emotion has impeded the helpful function of avoiding homelessness.)*

CLIENT: I don't want to leave. And if I start looking at places it is like saying I AM going to be evicted.

THERAPIST: Hmm, are you worried if your landlord found out you had another place to go he'd definitely throw you out? *(T. is aware the client is probably not being literal here, but chooses to take the worry seriously to keep modelling – your worries probably have some function, so look for the valid part first.)*

CLIENT: No, it's more that it makes it more real to me, you know, if I'm looking at other rentals.

THERAPIST: I totally get that; to plan for being evicted is like having to face your worst nightmare, so let's get that out of the way first, and the anxiety should reduce. Then we might be better at sorting things out with the landlord. *(T. validates, and suggests tackling the most feared solution first, as that is approaching rather than avoiding.)*

CLIENT: *(Reluctantly)* OK.

THERAPIST: Now it's going to help if we assume a body posture and facial expression with more confidence in it. Imagine your mate has asked you to help him move a piano, and you know it is going to be heavy. You've had the option to back out but decide to help. We want a body posture and face that say, 'OK, I'm up for this, let's DO IT'. *(T. coaches opposite action to anxiety in two domains, face and body posture. The use of metaphor helps the client identify appropriate actions.)*

CLIENT: *(Reluctantly straightens up in the chair, stops fidgeting.)*

THERAPIST: Head up, that's good, so let's think about options, what's your budget? *(Opens computer)* Let's look at some letting agencies. Here, pull your chair up, and start clicking down this list. *(T. activates 'approach' behaviour in solving the problem. Doing this in session allows T. to spot avoidant behaviours.)*

CLIENT: *(Moves forward, then looks away.)* Do I have to do this now? I have the internet at home.

THERAPIST: That might have been your mind urging you to avoid, so we need to be prepared for that to happen when we are regulating anxiety. Here's a tip – it might help to ask yourself this question – *in an hour's time, do I want this task in front of me or behind me?* And if the answer is, *'behind me'* then gently turn your mind back to what we are doing. I'll be guided by you on this, you can do it at home if you think it will be better. *(T. coaches mindfulness and highlights freedom to choose.)*

CLIENT: *(Looks back again, reluctantly)* But my flat is good value for money.

THERAPIST: Can we describe that more dialectically? That means referring to your current flat AND the potential new one? Keep your point, just bring in the idea that we now have two places to think about, where you are and where you might be moving to. *(T. spots a little polarised thinking here – there is just ONE good place – and encourages a dialectical position. Then invites behavioural rehearsal.)*

CLIENT: Er... I'd like it if the new flat was good value like mine. *(Looks at the screen)* These are expensive... *(Keeps looking)* ... Apart from these two, but they are small.

THERAPIST: Great! Take your time. Let me check, as you browse, is your anxiety going up or down? *(T. encourages the client to observe the trajectory of the emotion.)*

CLIENT: At first it went up... and now it's starting to drop.

THERAPIST: So mark down a couple of these rentals, and I will send you the links. Remember problem-solving doesn't prevent you from negotiating with the landlord, it just makes sure there is less riding on the outcome. *(T. summarises and clarifies the function of problem-solving.)* What's attracting your attention as you're browsing? *(T. is awake to the client's interest in the listings.)*

CLIENT: Places close to Mountford, ground floor with somewhere for my bike...This one looks a bit better than the others, but see the price...

THERAPIST: Yes, whenever you change rentals it's likely to be a higher price, what would you need to do to be able to afford it? *(T. avoids the urge to reassure or say, 'yes, but', and focusses on problem-solving the obstacle, another opposite action to anxiety.)*

CLIENT: I don't know. I'd have to cut down on what I spend. Though maybe if it's smaller, the bills would be lower. It's too much to think about.

THERAPIST: Those are good ideas. Your mind is saying 'don't have this problem'. Which is a bit like asking you not to be five foot ten. Keep turning in the right direction, towards the problem. Jot down the agent listing that property, and add any ideas about saving money and checking the cost of bills. *(T. highlights the internal escape behaviour and reinforces the slight movement into problem-solving.)*

CLIENT: *(Makes some notes)*

THERAPIST: Now I'm going to ask you a question. Going back to when you cut yourself yesterday, if you'd known you had other accommodation options, would you have been more likely to cut, or less likely? *(T. assesses the likely effects of this intervention on the target behaviour in the chain, i.e. cutting.)*

CLIENT: Depends where they were, but maybe less likely.

THERAPIST: OK, so we're on track. Now we can look at getting last night's anxiety down. What are the opposite actions for anxiety? Get your list out from group. *(T. activates behaviour to aid remembering.)*

CLIENT: *(Rummages in rucksack)* er... so if you're hot, cooling yourself down.

THERAPIST: How could you have cooled yourself last night? *(T. elicits behavioural rehearsal of 'opposite actions'.)*

CLIENT: Throw the bedcovers off, have a cold drink, splash my face with water, and *(reading)* it says here, 'long slow breathing'.

THERAPIST: Yes, let all the air out of your lungs, it's that out-breath that really helps. Do it now so I can see, and let your whole body sag – that will counter the tense muscles that go with anxiety. Smooth out those frown lines on your face, too. *(T. activates behavioural rehearsal to allow the client to feel the difference, and to check that the client is performing the skill correctly.)*

CLIENT: *(Rehearses breathing and relaxing the muscles, changing facial expression)* But a minute ago you were saying I had to do that piano thing, now you're telling me to relax.

THERAPIST: Good noticing. It's because opposite actions depend on the context. Earlier your anxiety was telling you to avoid looking at listings. You needed that piano-shifter confidence to help you act opposite and get problem-solving. But when you were getting to sleep, your anxiety was saying, *Why are you sleeping? You could be homeless any minute! Get up and sort your life out.* You needed some opposite action to get you more relaxed. *(T. explains the dialectical swings that are common in anxiety.)*

CLIENT: How will I know which to do?

THERAPIST: We have to work out what your anxiety is trying to get you to do, and whether that would be helpful or not. And sometimes you need a bit of both. Because there is a genuine threat of losing your home, we need to *keep* some anxiety. Although it's unpleasant, worrying about losing your home is entirely appropriate. Emotion regulation is about using your emotion to help you. So keep a notebook by your bed, and if you have a worry, write down some ideas for how you could start to solve it in the morning. Afterwards you can do the 'relaxing' type of opposite action. Last night, what would you have written in the notebook… *(T. wants to see the client has understood the skill.)*

CLIENT: Er… those property websites, remember that smaller places have smaller bills. *(This time the client comes more readily to the solutions.)*

THERAPIST: Great! Without some solutions relaxation won't work. Anxiety is trying to help you. Do you think if you'd have done that last night your urge to cut would have been higher or lower? *(T. checks the possible effect of the new behaviour on the target of cutting.)*

CLIENT: Lower. But it's hard to believe anxiety can ever be helpful.

THERAPIST: That's why we have to make friends with our emotions more, without letting them bully us. In a genuine problem we don't want to get your emotion down to zero. We need to keep the bit that matches the facts. Now we can go on to rehearse how you speak to the landlord if he broaches this topic again, maybe making your case for how the neighbours provoked you. I'll play the landlord and we can use your interpersonal effectiveness skills from group. They might not work, but then at least we have a plan B. *(T. summarises the steps in emotion regulation and they proceed to role-play some interpersonal effectiveness skills.)*

Special considerations in regulating anxiety and fear:

1) The strategies above are for when anxiety crops up as a link in the chain to a target behaviour. The intervention is for the purpose of teaching context-based regulation skills and enhancing emotional literacy. A diagnosed anxiety disorder should be treated with the appropriate evidence-based protocols.

2) Anxiety confuses therapists because the action urge for anxiety is to avoid, which is an opposite action in itself. Clinicians tie themselves in knots trying to work out what exactly to act opposite to. My tip, as in the scenario, is to establish (a) what the person feels like doing and (b) if that would be helpful or not.

3) Anxiety feeds off itself, because the urge to avoid the prompting event (e.g. I don't want to be homeless) quickly transforms into an urge to avoid the sensations of anxiety (I don't want to feel anxious about being homeless). Clients often prioritise avoiding the feeling over solving the problem.

4) When the client is confronted with the thing they have most anxiety about (in this case the property listings) they can flip into pure fear; so they become pale, get cold and are inactive. This is not resistance, but a physiological response like a rabbit caught in the headlights. It should pass with a little validation.

5) The cure for inappropriate anxiety and fear is exposure to the feared thing, essentially acting opposite to the urge to run away or avoid. There is a list of symptom induction tests in Barlow's seminal text *Anxiety and It's Disorders* that bring home how important opposite action is in treatment – e.g. if the client fears feeling dizzy, spinning them around in a chair, if they fear a racing heart, having them run on the spot (Barlow 2002 pgs 344–346). Heidi asked me to read this book at the start of my DBT career and I would urge you to do the same.

6) It is hard for a therapist to go towards what clients fear (e.g. maintaining a concerned facial expression) when the urge is to reassure. There is no need to go over the top – we are not trying to terrify the client. But some portrayal of the emotion is helpful to model that you can be anxious and you don't die. The trick is to stop the client spinning off into predicting catastrophe.

7) Pure fear kicks in when the danger is much closer, and running away is not an option. It is a cold emotion so the client needs warming up. The action urge is to freeze, so expect that the client will respond and react slowly. The theory of regulating pure fear is exactly the same as for anxiety – some domains are different, e.g. temperature and action urges. The therapist has to activate movement to counter the inaction, whereas in anxiety they have to inhibit the client's urge to run away.

8) Of all the emotions anxiety has the worst rap, with clients and therapists automatically assuming it must be reduced or eliminated, instead of treated like any other emotion.

When does fear need up-regulating?

If the client is behaving in a dangerous way with scant regard for the consequences, they might need more fear. An adolescent client would ride passenger when her friends illegally raced their cars on public roads. She knew it was unsafe. But the thrill of being with them and having fun was too great to decline. Afterwards she would think, 'I can't believe we did that, it was dumb, we could have been killed'. But then she would accept the next invitation. Her therapist got her to rehearse the moment when she was invited to get into the car, adding in the signature features of fear – tensing her muscles, shortening her breathing, furrowing her brow, while imagining the danger. The hope is that this will trigger a more instinctive self-protection response when presented with the same cue. In my own experience, rehearsing signature features where the emotion is missing takes much longer to create an effect than opposite actions. It might take months, before the person starts to notice a more spontaneous response.

Reference

Barlow, D. H. (2002). *Anxiety and its disorders*, 2nd ed. New York, NY: Guilford.

CHAPTER

9 | Joy

When does joy fit the facts?

Joy fits the facts when there is a potential gain or benefit for the individual.

In the joy family: Happiness, love, delight, pleasure, gladness, enthusiasm, passion, thrill, excitement, humour, love.

Action urges: To repeat that action, do more of the thing that sparked joy.

Function of the emotion: To maximise benefits, to increase achievements.

Signature features of joy

- **Temperature:** Warm
- **Facial expression:** Open, eyebrows up, smiling, laughing
- **Breathing:** Fast
- **Muscle tone:** Springy
- **Voice tone:** Light, high

- **Posture:** Expansive
- **Gesture:** Focussed upwards, pumping the air, swinging the arms, a bounce in the step
- **Overt actions**: Dancing, clapping, relaxing, increased speed and energy, increased interactions.

Joy example scenario

In the following example the client is in her early 20s and has been working on reducing her self-harm, along with her cannabis and co-caine use. She is hoping to get back into education as she is bitterly disappointed with her current lifestyle. She lives alone in a ground floor flat and had successfully avoided some cannabis-dealing friends, until the previous weekend, when she let them into her flat. She ended up using cocaine then harming herself.

THERAPIST: So you were lying in bed around lunchtime and heard a rap on your window? *(T. establishes the context.)*

CLIENT: Yes, the window is by my bed, I pushed back the curtain and saw Ari and K-J, two of the guys who go to Cellar 9 (a local drinking place.) They'd pushed through the hedge at the back of the flats when they saw my curtains were closed. I hadn't seen them since I've been staying away from the Cellar. I've only self-harmed once in those four weeks. When I looked out Ari was there grinning at me. I told them to go round to the front.

THERAPIST: Fantastic about not cutting. So what was going through your mind at that moment when you said, 'Go round'? *(T. reinforces goal-relevant behaviour and continues to gather links in the chain of events.)*

CLIENT: I like them *(shrugs)* even though I've been trying to stay away. If we could've just gone for coffee it would have been fine. I shouldn't have let them in… *(pauses)*. Ari's stupid grin... I don't know... It was just nice that they wanted to see me.

THERAPIST: It's perfectly natural that you would be pleased to see them, and to feel happy that they wanted to see you. We all like to think people will go out of their way for us. So if you had to name that emotion from our list? *(T. validates the emotion and pulls for the first part of the skill, emotion labelling.)*

CLIENT: Joy... but they didn't go out of their way, they'd been out all night at a party and were just walking back through the estate. They know I draw my curtains when I'm up, so they guessed I'd be in.

THERAPIST: They could've walked on by... but OK, so you had a surge of joy, and then... *(T. repeats the name of the emotion and goes back to eliciting the chain of events.)*

CLIENT: I jumped out of bed and threw on some clothes, went to the door and that was that. I didn't even try and stop them coming in. They stayed all day, ate my food, bummed money off me, and I ended up doing weed and cocaine, and then thinking WHY DO I DO THIS??? I KNEW what would happen...

THERAPIST: Maybe because when you saw them you were affected by that surge of joy. We call this *mood dependent behaviour*. You wanted to see them so you let them in, that makes complete sense even if a little voice in your head is saying, 'don't do it'. But I CAN help you loosen the grip of the emotion if you want. Not so that you can be mean to them, but so you can maybe suggest coffee rather than letting them in. *(T. validates the client's mood-drive response, and seeks an invitation to treat.)*

CLIENT: Yes please.

THERAPIST: Let's go back to the emotion regulation teaching from group, when does Joy fit the facts? *(T. elicits an active response from client in the skill of 'checking the facts')*

CLIENT: When er. something is good for you? I mean, if it's a benefit. But seriously? It was a disaster!

THERAPIST: Let's not dismiss the emotion so quickly, what was the main source of your joy? *(T. reminds the client to validate the part of the emotion that is justified before moving to down-regulate.)*

CLIENT: It was that they remembered me and wanted to see me.

THERAPIST: Yes, the social aspects. So even if you didn't want them to come in, your emotion is telling you that you like friendly company, as we all do. That is an important message about yourself. *(T. models that emotions contain information about the self.)*

CLIENT: I'd rather it wasn't Ari and K-J, though. They're ok in small doses, you know what I mean?

THERAPIST: Yes, it's two ends of the dialectic. But if not them, then you need to make some new friends to hang out with on Saturdays.

CLIENT: It's not easy...

THERAPIST: It's one of the hardest things of all, so maybe start now while you're in DBT so I can help you. We can draw up a list of 'friend-recruiting behaviours' – for instance, some of the dating apps now have a 'friendship' section, too – to meet people for social events. *(T. pulls for problem-solving the valid part of the emotion.)*

CLIENT: I bet YOU don't have any friends. Anyone who says, 'Friend-recruiting behaviours' is such a loser.

THERAPIST: *(Writing)* Ah, *'good sense of humour'*, there we go! That's your profile started... *(T. uses irreverence to derail the client's diversionary tactics.)* What else can go on our list? Give me at least two more things you are going to do.

CLIENT: *(Sighing)* OK, I will look at one of those 'sad-loser' apps. And... whatever, I'm not going to the gym, I'm not in good shape.

THERAPIST: *(Playful tone)* Argh! more *mindful descriptions*, pur-leeeese! Calling it a sad-loser app is not going to motivate you. Anyway, you don't have to solely meet *new* people, you can reconnect with people you knew a while back, maybe slightly more healthy relationships than at Cellar 9. Are there any friends you don't see any more that you could drop an email or text? *(T. lightly challenges language, but does not demand to see the behaviour as the client is moving the right way. T. looks for avenues the client might be missing.)*

CLIENT: *(Grumbling)* I can think of a couple of people I've seen since school, but not recently. I don't know... won't it be weird to just hear from me out of the blue?

THERAPIST: People like to be remembered, they like to know someone went out of their way to get in touch... sound familiar? *(T. revisits the function of the emotion, the benefit of social connection.)*

CLIENT: Oh Ha Ha. you're SO clever. *(Big sigh)* OK, I'll do it. But there's no point if I keep letting Ari and K-J in, so shall we get on with that?

THERAPIST: OK, let's go back to the moment you push back the curtain and feel that surge of joy. *(T. revisits the context of the emotional incident.)* We know we don't want to send them away, but we can reduce the joy so you suggest coffee rather than letting them in. One signature feature of joy is the eyebrow flash, particularly on greeting. So would you be willing to just keep your eyebrows down? Not a frown, just don't raise them? Imagine pushing back the curtain and let's practise the low-brow greeting. *(T. activates new facial expression as a form of behavioural rehearsal.)*

CLIENT: *(Complies)* That feels really weird.

THERAPIST: Less or more joyful?

CLIENT: Less.

THERAPIST: Let's rehearse then, pretend you are sitting up in bed. Now, rushing is a signature of joy, and my guess is that you rushed to the door. You could sit on the side of your bed and pause for a minute. And do you think you could keep your face slightly more neutral. Don't frown because that would deny the bit of you that's happy to see them, just tone it down a bit. Now pretend you are walking to the door and show me a less springy walk. *(T. activates behavioural rehearsal of opposite action to joy.)*

CLIENT: (Tuts and eyerolls, then rehearses doing everything more slowly, with a neutral facial expression.)

THERAPIST: Hmm, increase the joy a little, you can still smile, but don't grin. We want to match the facts – you're pleased to see them, but want to go for coffee, not invite them in. *(T. coaches more nuanced regulation, ignoring the huffing and puffing as the client is doing as required. Many behaviours like sighing, eyerolling, or tutting function to down-regulate anxiety.)*

CLIENT: This feels really stupid.

THERAPIST: (Brightly) That's the spirit! *(T. uses irreverence rather than a direct challenge.)*

CLIENT: *(Laughs)* Don't make me laugh then. Hmmph. How about this (rehearses the face again)

THERAPIST: What's happening to the joy? Does it feel more like the coffee-shop version or are we still offering open-house to them? *(T. assesses the consequences of the new behaviour.)*

CLIENT: I don't feel as happy, but surely that's because I am here with you and not lonely at home being glad to see my old mates? So how would that work on the actual day?

THERAPIST: OK, imagine you're pushing back the curtain and show me exactly the same face and actions as you did that day, eyebrows up, bouncy walk, etc. If our theory is correct it will feel *more* joyful, even though you are still only in the presence of sad-loser me. *(T. suggests a behavioural experiment for comparison purposes.)*

CLIENT: *(Complies, becomes thoughtful)* Yeah, I guess it does feel different. I guess I can try it.

THERAPIST: Now the last thing is your tone of voice at the door. We don't want a harsh tone or words, because that would invalidate your delight at seeing them, but we want to reduce the joy in your tone a bit, so that you are less likely to let them in. *(T. coaches a dialectical approach to choosing voice tone – how much lightness is too much, how much is not enough. T. refers back to the valid function of the emotion.)*

CLIENT: Well, what I actually said was, 'Hi, Ari, you muppet, you nearly broke my window?' and I was laughing.

THERAPIST: OK, so what would still be friendly but not imply 'we're great mates' *(T. pulls for discernment skills)* and maybe have a suggestion ready for what you'd like to happen next, so that they don't get to set the agenda? *(T. coaches 'cope ahead'.)*

CLIENT: I don't know.

THERAPIST: Just think about it, take your time, how do you want it to go? You can work it out. *(T. gives time for reflection to strengthen the client's sense of self. This is a form of wise mind.)*

CLIENT: I don't know... OK... maybe saying, 'Hi guys, I'm just going to grab a decent coffee at the shop, want to come?'

THERAPIST: Perfect! Let's put it all together from when the curtain goes back... Taddah! See what I did there? 'When the curtain goes back', you know, like in a theatre! *(T. activates behavioural rehearsal.)*

CLIENT: You are so lame. (Conducts the behavioural rehearsal.)

THERAPIST: OK, if you had done that on the day, do you think you'd have been more likely or less likely to end up harming yourself? *(T. assesses the consequences of the new behaviours on the target behaviour.)*

CLIENT: I think less likely, but I need to give it a go at home.

Special considerations in regulating joy

1) Therapists can be reluctant to down-regulate joy, given that our clients often lead lives devoid of much pleasure. It should be viewed as any other emotion and not assumed to be positive. For example, clients in prison or in-patient units often experience joy when seeing others in pain or distress.

2) In the scenario above the therapist was able to be quite jokey, as that matched the context. A dour therapist teaching joy-reducing techniques has low appeal, for anyone. The therapist ignores the light-hearted insults, as the client is complying with coaching. (Therapists can also use humour as an irreverent strategy when the client is very serious, to shift the mood.)

3) Inappropriate joy is often seen in a chain towards addictive behaviours, where it probably appears early on, as a vulnerability factor. For example, with compulsive shopping the client may get joy when putting her purse in her bag to go to the shop, or opening up the shopping app on her phone. In the example above the joy required some regulation before the client reached the front door, where she could activate the decision to keep the friends out of the flat.

4) The manic phase of a bi-polar episode is technically inappropriate joy, and will respond to opposite action in the same way. However, during a manic phase cognitive processes can be more disrupted, as hormones and blood chemistry are affected. For example in the scenario above the client originally acted in the grip of joy and let the two guys in, but still had access to the cognition 'this is not really a great idea'. In a delusional mania the client may lack this insight, and therefore be less motivated to change.

5) Linehan separates love and joy, but I like to say that love is in the joy family, a pleasurable feeling denoting benefit. Sometimes people love others where there is no personal gain. In this case love might fit the facts if there was a 'kinship' gain – e.g. the wellbeing of a dependent or family member. On the other hand we often find people accepting cruel treatment in the name of love. If this happens check out whether this is actually separation anxiety rather than love. For example, *'I don't like being with this person but feel bad when we are apart'*. Or it might be a phobia of grieving – *'I don't want to be sad when we separate so we must stay together'* or even a fear of aloneness, *'I think this is the best relationship I can get'*. Some people are so unused to being cared for that they assume love IS pain, *'If it doesn't hurt it can't be love'*. Linehan (2015b pg 253) urges people to end destructive relationships and to do so often involves acting opposite to the actions that signify loving.

When does joy need up-regulating?

One example is where the client complains of being numb or distracted during an activity that would normally promote joy. For example, a client who does not live with her children but has access to visits finds she is plagued by the thought of having to return them to their carer and is unable to connect with the pleasure of seeing them.

Another example is when a client has depressed episodes, though beware – increasing pleasurable activities is not the same as up-regulating joy. Up-regulating refers to increasing the emotion where someone might naturally feel it (so it would match the facts) but it is absent. For example, depressed clients frequently experience lack of pleasure during sexual activity, and can find it embarrassing to talk about or shameful to admit. Although this is also the case with people who have sexual abuse histories I find they are slightly more likely to tell their therapist because it is understandable. By contrast depressed clients sometimes hold the attitude that getting sexual pleasure would feel like a luxury, with more important things to focus on like getting back to work, or paying the bills. This is really self-invalidating, and as this whole book is about the mind-body link we should not underestimate the psychological distress caused by loss of sexual pleasure, even if our clients are dismissive. Therapists can refer the client to organisations like Relate or sexual dysfunction clinics for specialist help.

Joy can also be upregulated if the client lacks motivation to do a desired task. For example, a client who wants to tidy a cluttered garage. A fine dry day comes along with nothing else in the diary, but it still seems like a chore. The therapist might coach acting opposite to the slumped shoulders and that tone of voice that says, 'Oh no, I will have to spend the whole day humping dusty boxes'. An alternative might be for the client to say in a more up-beat voice; 'OK, I don't feel like tidying AND at the same time I would really like a tidy garage'. To change posture and even just walk purposefully towards the garage rather than stay in the kitchen. Attending to the start of the action is sometimes the key, focussing on the present rather than rehearsing the misery of the entire task. Encourage the client to go down to the garage and stand in it as if they are going to tidy it, without thinking any further than that, and see what happens.

10 Guilt

When does guilt fit the facts?

Guilt fits the facts when the person has violated a group rule or norm, but to an extent that does not risk being expelled from the group.

In the guilt family: Being to blame, responsible, at fault, in the wrong.

Action urges: To make a repair. Where a client describes the action urge as being 'to punish myself' this is normally a learned response from a childhood where guilt only ended when a culprit had been identified and punished. Self-punishment is therefore a corruption of the natural action urge, and is driven by a desire to hasten the ending of that guilty feeling.

Function of the emotion: To ensure the person stays connected with the tribe in order to benefit from the resources and protection offered by a group.

Signature features of guilt

- **Temperature:** Uncomfortably warm.

- **Facial expression:** Teeth slightly parted, behind closed lips. A characteristic of guilt is bowing the head in supplication, but in order to check the response from the other person the eyes and eyebrows lift, giving a signature centre-brow raise. Increased guilt may mean total avoidance of eye contact.

- **Breathing:** Slows (not drawing attention to self) and into upper chest as the shoulders are raised.

- **Muscle tone:** Moderate tension.

- **Voice tone:** Feeling guilty probably inhibits someone from saying very much. But an apologetic tone has a recognisable supplication in it. When people have no 'appealing tone' in their voice their apologies are often considered insincere. Just raising the eyebrows in the centre during an apology can change the voice tone to sound more heartfelt.

- **Posture:** Shoulders raised, making oneself smaller in supplication, head may angle down to the side.

- **Gesture:** Shoulders are sometimes raised and dropped during an appeal, with an open-hand gesture to signify acceptance of guilt. Gives rise to expressions like 'Guilty shrug' or 'I hold my hands up'. Shifting position or squirming.

- **Overt actions:** Apologising, avoiding people or places that retrigger the guilt.

Guilt example scenario

In the following example the client is in addiction therapy. He works in advertising and prepared a presentation on a new product with a colleague, who fell ill before it was due, but encouraged him to go ahead without her. The client changed the content of the presentation and removed his colleague's name. Later that evening he had the urge to drink.

THERAPIST: So after the presentation you had the urge to drink? *(T. seeks clarification on timings.)*

CLIENT: No, it was later that evening, when I got home, I spoke to Maxine on the phone and she asked how it had gone. I told her it went well – and it had done. I told her I'd made one or two tweaks. The thing is, I really had to do a lot of work to make it a success. And I couldn't ask her to help because she was ill. I improved it massively. It was not even the same presentation when I had finished. The audience were keen on the product, so that's all that matters. She will benefit financially from that as well as me. It was straight after the call, I had the urge to drink.

THERAPIST: Ah, so it seems the call had gone well? Was there an emotion around at that moment? *(T. shapes the skill of emotion labelling.)*

CLIENT: I had this wave of guilt, but there was no need. I changed it enough, so that legitimately the work was my own. She should be grateful to me really. She was ill with stress, so I was protecting her. And there was no need to tell her that I took her name off, because it would just have rubbed her nose in it.

THERAPIST: OK, well maybe we can down-regulate that guilt then. Do you remember when guilt fits the facts? It's really to keep you in with the group. So moving away from the outcome, do you think there was any group norm or rule that you had violated between you and Maxine? *(T. reminds the client of the function of the emotion, and coaches 'check the facts'.)*

CLIENT: Erm, I'm not sure. I suppose we do a lot of presentations together, so there was a sense of shared ownership, but on this occasion, first she wasn't attending, second I did everything myself, to give the customer what they wanted.

THERAPIST: It sounds like you worked hard on that presentation. And thinking back, do you have your own theory about the guilt? Do you think it related to taking her name off the materials? Or that you didn't mention it to her? *(T. validates the hard work, and coaches the client to be curious about the emotion. Asking, "do you have a theory?" Leaves the control with the client, particularly helpful if there is a chance of them feeling judged.)*

CLIENT: She never asked me if her name was on there, so I didn't lie.

THERAPIST: That's fine, take your time, we might not be able to work it out, but if you have a hunch... *(because this is a potentially painful cue, the therapist allows plenty of time for the client to access the emotion).*

CLIENT: Well, it did cross my mind she might ask to see the presentation. It would have been easy to pass off an earlier version that we'd done together. But then I felt awful because, what kind of person would even think of doing that? I mean she encouraged me to do the pitch without her. We could have postponed. And if she found out I'd lied she would have had nothing to do with me ever again.

THERAPIST: So it sounds as though you avoided doing something that might have been shameful, and risked you being expelled from that relationship. *(T. clarifies the difference between guilt and shame.)*

CLIENT: I felt bad about even considering it.

THERAPIST: You are being hard on yourself, you can't be blamed for thoughts that you DON'T act on! *(The client looks doubtful. T. continues in a matter-of-fact tone.)* So was there anything you did that you feel violated the unspoken agreements between you? *(T. returns to the function of the emotion.)*

CLIENT: It was taking her name off, and knowing she'd believe I'd kept it on. I didn't lie, I just didn't own up.

THERAPIST: OK. Well, people often assume that a feeling of guilt means they must be a 'bad' person, whereas really, feeling guilty shows that you have a conscience. There are some people who might have told a barefaced lie about this, and fooled her with that previous version without batting an eye-lid. Their only priority would be not getting caught. That would be the guilt-free version. *(T. clarifies the function of the emotion.)*

CLIENT: That makes me feel better.

THERAPIST: And at the same time the action urge for guilt is to make a repair. So what damage do you think was done to Maxine when you omitted her name without telling her? *(T. shapes the client's ability to recognise problem-solving as a solution.)*

CLIENT: Well obviously she can't rely on me... I'm totally selfish. I can't be trusted... *(Squirms in the seat, shakes his head.)*

THERAPIST: I can see that weighs heavily on you, yet you didn't go so far as to lie. Try lowering your shoulders and lifting your head to lower the guilt a bit. So the violation was that you usually work together and although she'd encouraged you to pitch you had not put her name on the presentation, and didn't tell her? Is that about right?

CLIENT: The worst thing is she would have expected some expo-sure for herself. We work in advertising so we are building our personal reputation as well as that of the company. I know that presentation made me look good, so... I'm a ter-rible person.

THERAPIST: It sounds like your guilt fits the facts to some degree, but when you say 'I'm a terrible person' How high does it go?

CLIENT: 110%.

THERAPIST: You didn't murder her, or even murder her reputa-tion, so how high do you think this action warrants. Trying to discern where this would sit compared to say, other cut-throat things that happen in advertising?

CLIENT: It's hard. Maybe 40%?

THERAPIST: And thinking about how to repair this, how aggrieved do you think she would have been if you had owned up? *(T. doesn't argue about the level, because the client was previously rating at 110% so has come down a lot. The ability to change the level is what matters.)*

CLIENT: She can be quite fiery, although she tries to play right by most people. She's been annoyed at me before and still helped me with my promotion. I owe her a lot actually. But she's not perfect herself, you know.

THERAPIST: Very dialectical – everyone is a 'work in progress'! So let's go back to how much guilt we want to keep, and think of a repair you would need to do to make it up to her. *(T. validates and encourages problem-solving.)*

CLIENT: Are you saying I have to own up?

THERAPIST: Hmm… interesting question! In DBT we try not to say you HAVE to do anything, instead we ask, what would be the most effective thing to do right now? If you do nothing at all, probably this guilt will just go down and you will forget this incident, unless she finds out later. So you could just wait for that to happen. It depends whether a guilty secret would affect how you work together. It could make you nicer to her, or make you want to avoid her. But there is another issue, which is how this effects your sense of self. Generally our self-view suffers if we know we have done something against our values and haven't tried to put it right. On the other hand, we don't want to over-apologise, because that also saps our self-esteem. You need to choose a response that fits in with these dialectical tensions. To do enough, not too little and not too much. *(T. explains what taking a dialectical approach would mean in this instance.)*

CLIENT: I absolutely hate feeling like I am to blame, that's why I wanted to drink. But if I try to repair this I have to say I was in the wrong. I don't like either of those options.

THERAPIST: Hmmm. Remember this was not the end of the world. If your guilt shoots up to an unmanageable level maybe you are adding in guilt about other things you have done. Sometimes if you have a history of substance misuse you are very sensitive to things that have caused guilt in the past. *(T. validates the reluctance by suggesting some controlling variables.)*

CLIENT: Like all the things I did that contributed to my marriage breaking up? The advertising industry is really stressful, and the whole culture revolves around drinking. I screwed up in so many different ways...

THERAPIST: Whoa, that makes perfect sense as to why you are sensitive to guilt. So we need to be mindful, just this one incident, this one moment. Hold your body a little more upright, don't drop your head, Try mindfully describing, 'I let Maxine down by removing her name, and I feel guilty for not telling her, and at the same time, I made a larger contribution to this project'. *(T. coaches mindfulness and a dialectical stance.)*

CLIENT: *(Repeats the phrase.)* That doesn't feel as bad as I thought.

THERAPIST: Yes, you kept a fairly composed face and didn't get defensive. The idea is that we can touch the truth of the matter without being either overwhelmed or dismissive. This is emotional literacy. *(T. coaches a dialectical approach.)*

CLIENT: So do I have to own up to Maxine?

THERAPIST: I can't say because you need to ask yourself that question. It is your own emotion that you are solving, here, so check in with your wise mind. Are there other ways to repair what has been broken? It's not just about owning up. *(T. encourages the client to evaluate their emotion regulation strategies, and look for what has been left out.)*

CLIENT: Er... I suppose I could get back to the company we pitched to... and... bring Maxine's name to their attention.

THERAPIST: Can you do that without compromising the deal? *(T. models solution evaluation.)*

CLIENT: Yes, I can send across some supplementary materials and put her name uppermost. If I did that I would then feel better about owning up to Maxine, because I could say, 'I did this thing that I feel guilty about, and so these are the steps I have taken to put it right'.

THERAPIST: Sounds like a plan. What do you think she would say if you did that? *(T. encourages some 'cope ahead' skills.)*

CLIENT: She won't be pleased, but she will be less mad at me.

THERAPIST: And how does it fit with your own values. I mean, we started out with you telling me you had nothing to feel guilty for, and now we have moved to making some kind of repair to Maxine. You need to evaluate for yourself, does it feel like a wise action. *(T. encourages the client to check the effectiveness of the skill. This helps strengthen the sense of self.)*

CLIENT: It feels much more comfortable.

THERAPIST: So we have learnt today that even an unpleasant emotion is probably telling us something important, and even when we don't like that message, we can feel better if we listen to it and act on it. But first we have to work out how much, roughly, is appropriate. *(T. summarises the essence of emotional regulation.)*

CLIENT: *(Thoughtfully)* You know, I've always felt as though guilt is hovering there in the background ready to pounce on me for all the bad things I've done. That if I let myself feel it I'd be opening the floodgate. I've worried that people will only see my faults. But just being mindful about this one incident, it's been... well, I didn't think you could break it down like that. I thought it was all or nothing, if you were guilty you were a bad person.

THERAPIST: Dialectics help us move away from those extremes. So if on that day you could have assessed your guilt level, worked out how much fitted the facts, and then devised a strategy for repairing the damage, would you have felt more like drinking or less like it? *(T. assesses the impact of these solutions on the target behaviour.)*

CLIENT: I'm not sure. I hate feeling guilty so much, so maybe not... but then... it's interesting that you can repair... And I definitely feel better now about Maxine, so I'm coming round to the idea.

THERAPIST: You're right, it's not a quick fix, it takes practice. *(T. validates and allows the client's own pacing, this will crop up again during therapy, it's not a race, but incremental changes.)*

Special considerations in regulating guilt

1) Fear of feeling guilty is often worse for clients than the guilt itself. Half the battle is encouraging willingness to go towards the emotion. It helps to point out, as in this example, that the experience of guilt is not a measure of badness.

2) The cognitive aspects of guilt are probably stronger than the physiological, as the signature features are subtle. What the client is saying to him or herself about their guilt is very important.

3) Clients and therapists can fall into the trap of dealing with past guilt – e.g. in this scenario changing the discussion to include the marital incidents. I encourage therapists to trust the process and work on the *current* incident of guilt. Do not be deflected even if past guilt seems huge.

4) Although Linehan says guilt is when you have violated your own values, you may need an external point of reference to truly establish whether the emotion fits the facts. For example, a girl with an eating disorder who feels guilty for eating a single apple will tell you she HAS gone against her own

values (but clearly guilt does not fit the facts.) Or someone who has stolen a pensioner's life savings might say they
have not violated a single value of theirs (when clearly guilt
would fit the facts.) This is why it is better to ask, is there a
group norm that you have broken?

5) Clients sometimes belong to groups that have dysfunctional
norms, such as pro-anorexia, or hyper-critical social groups.
They might need to radically change their social circle.

6) If the person to whom repair is owed is absent or deceased,
the client may need help to find a substitute repair – to a
charity or other person who represents the issue. For example, 'I felt guilty because it was the anniversary of my grandmother's death and I never visited her in hospital'. A repair
might be enacted by asking the client to state out loud what
they wanted to say to their grandmother, or by donating to a
charity for the elderly, or befriending another older person.
A creative approach is needed.

7) In the scenario above the client began with a number of
defensive statements. On the surface these may look like an
absence of guilt but usually denote the opposite – a sensitivity to being blamed. If guilt is genuinely absent it would
not even occur to the client to defend themselves against it.

8) Psychopaths can experience a complete absence of guilt
(one once told me, I could break the chair arm or *your* arm
and it would be the same to me.) Be very wary of teaching
true psychopaths how to 'fake' guilt. This just makes them
more effective predators. Take any doubts you may have to
your DBT consultation meeting.

9) Linehan notes how many BPD clients are overly sensitive to
guilt, and end up apologising for everything. In her interpersonal effectiveness handouts on the FAST skills (for keeping
your self-respect) (Linehan 2015b pg 130) she urges clients
to limit those apologies.

When does guilt need up-regulating?

Guilt needs up-regulating if the client is engaging in behaviours that cause damage or distress to others and makes no sign of wanting to make a repair. For example, taking or breaking the possessions of others, damaging property, being casual with other people's confidential information. Interestingly, guilt can sometimes need up-regulating to increase motivation to accomplish a task. If, e.g. someone has failed to fill in their diary card for the third week running, or agreed to an assignment and not done it, the therapist might say, 'Would it be helpful to have a little guilt about this?'

It is hard to up-regulate guilty behaviours, because as stated previously, bodily manifestations of guilt are subtle. If the client can accurately outline the impact of their behaviour whilst reducing defensiveness this is a good start. In the following scenario the client had the urge to harm himself when he thought he was guilty, but then when he was not, his urge went away. The therapist works on exposure to the feeling of guilt.

THERAPIST: So at first you thought that you had left the tap running and flooded the art-room floor, then Ria said she had been in there after you?

CLIENT: Yes, it was such a relief, my urge went away immediately.

THERAPIST: Great that you didn't want to harm yourself, and at the same time, I'm worried that if you had been guilty you would have cut your arm. Would it be helpful to you to practise feeling guilty and just repairing? *(T. seeks an invitation to treat.)*

CLIENT: I'd rather just be more careful in the art room.

THERAPIST: *(Laughs)* and just generally all-round perfect, huh? What are the chances? *(T. Uses irreverence to make the point that guilt cannot be avoided.)*

125

CLIENT: Hmm…

THERAPIST: So we could, if you are willing, have you practised saying to the art teacher, 'Oh dear, I was the one who left the tap running', and accepting the feeling at about the right level, I'm just interested in whether it sky-rockets, and if it does I can help you with that. *(T. gives a rationale for this work, and pulls for behavioural rehearsal.)*

CLIENT: But I know it wasn't me.

THERAPIST: Ah, yes, I can see that. Can you imagine being back before you knew? *(T. validates by taking the obstacle seriously. Then suggests a solution.)*

CLIENT: I'll try… erm. 'It was actually me who left the tap on…'

THERAPIST: How's that feeling? On a scale of 0–100. *(T. encourages the client to assess the effect on their emotion.)*

CLIENT: 50%, and uncomfortable. I'm just thinking of the damage, and how I should've been more careful.

THERAPIST: I can see you've kind of shrunk into your shoulders. Do the opposite action and pull yourself a bit more upright, which will also cool you down slightly, as guilt is a warm emotion. To see how much guilt fits the facts we need to know the damage? *(T. knows this client avoids guilt, so at the same time as coaching opposite action, is also allowing the client to experience feeling guilty, by asking about the damage.)*

CLIENT: Some paint containers and boxes of paper got spoiled, and the floor needed mopping. Fortunately nobody's work was stored on the floor, we always have to put it on racks or easels, I think they have had floods before.

THERAPIST: Great fact-checking, there. So posture upright, voice firm, and maybe add an apology and offer to help. We want to acknowledge the actions that led to the damage, but not too much guilt because they were not deliberate. *(T. coaches a dialectical approach, with some opposite action where the guilt is too strong.)*

CLIENT: *(Complies)* 'Sorry I left the tap on, what can I do to help?' I suppose instead of asking, I could just grab some cloths and start mopping up?

THERAPIST: Much better, I'm wondering whether it feels bearable, without an urge to hurt yourself? *(T. checks the intervention against the target behaviour.)*

CLIENT: It's hard to say, because I know I was not to blame. But it made me think, what if it was my fault? It's really strange to practise just saying sorry and helping out. Before, I only wanted to stop feeling bad. I can see why you got me to do it. I didn't have any urges, because it wasn't factual. It was still worth doing, though.

THERAPIST: Linehan says learn to love your emotion, yet why would anyone love feeling guilty? Because you can feel proud that doing damage matters to you and allow your guilt to motivate you to put things right. So much better to feel it, assess it, repair it, then forget it. You can hold your head up at the end of that process. *(T. describes the dialectical paradox that allowing yourself to feel the emotion is also a method of getting it to go away.)*

Reference

Linehan, M. (2015b). *DBT skills training handouts and worksheets*, 2nd ed. New York, London: Guilford Publications.

11 Shame

When does shame fit the facts?

Shame fits the facts when someone has violated a group rule or norm to such an extent that if the group were aware of the transgression there is a risk that he or she would be expelled.

In the shame family: Humiliated, mortified, remorseful, conscience-stricken.

Action urges: The person will experience the desire to hide themselves or their 'crime'.

Function of the emotion: Historically there are many benefits of being in a tribe, including protection from threat and the pooling of resources. The urge to hide would lower the risk of being cast out, and also allow time for the issue to blow over.

Signature features of shame

- **Temperature:** Hot
- **Facial expression:** Downcast, angled away from others, avoidance of eye contact

- **Breathing:** Slow and into upper chest area
- **Muscle tone**: Varying between loose tone and tensing on approach by others
- **Voice tone:** Reluctant speech
- **Posture:** Curling, shrinking, or turning away
- **Gesture:** Covering the face
- **Overt actions:** Locking oneself away, refusing to meet with others, acts of self-denigration.

Shame example scenario

In the following example the client reports having an urge to harm herself after watching a TV documentary about people on benefits, which was very negative. She used to be a care assistant, and due to mental health problems has been unable to return to work.

THERAPIST: So did you have the urge to harm yourself during the programme, or only afterwards. *(T. assesses the timing of the urge.)*

CLIENT: After the programme. I just thought that this is how people see me, as some kind of scrounger. But I used to work SO hard. Caring for older people is physically exhausting as well as all the emotional stuff.

THERAPIST: It takes every bit of your resources to do a job like that, it's a heart and soul job. So it must have been a real shock to see that documentary. And what was the emotion? *(T. validates, and pulls for the skill of emotional identification.)*

CLIENT: I think a mixture of sadness and shame

THERAPIST: I can see the logic for both of those, and they are painful to feel. So if you had to say which one was more powerful in driving that urge, which would it be? *(T. is shaping the client's emotional literacy by first reinforcing the labelling of affect, and second giving the message that we regulate ONE emotion at a time.)*

CLIENT: It was the shame.

THERAPIST: OK, so do you remember how to check the facts for shame? *(T. pulls for the next stage in emotion regulation, 'check the facts'.)*

CLIENT: I know... it's to do with... whether the group would reject you, and it would, that's exactly what that programme was all about.

THERAPIST: Right, so there is definitely an element of your shame that is trying to protect you *(T. refers to the evolutionary benefits of shame. This is important because many clients have the idea that if they feel shame it means they are a very bad person, rather than it being a throwback to an evolutionary defence mechanism.)*

CLIENT: So you're saying I SHOULD be ashamed?

THERAPIST: Actually the shame is really telling us more about the nature of the *group*, than about you. It was telling us something about a certain section of society that either made or watched that programme and agreed with the judgemental stance that it took. We want to keep hold of the 'truth' that some people ARE judgemental, because that is honouring the emotional response you had. Most emotions happen for a reason, and this one is telling you, 'look out, there are people who would reject you just for being on benefits'. *(T. highlights the emotion's function, moving away from any judgements about what should or should not happen.)*

CLIENT: It's so unfair.

THERAPIST: I agree, it sounds as though the documentary was very one-sided, which is the opposite of being dialectical. So we might want to look at the other side, that not all of society's views were represented last night. *(T. validates the client's response, and models a dialectical stance.)*

CLIENT: That's fine here with you, but last night, I felt like every-one was against me.

THERAPIST: Yes, when an emotion takes hold, it throws everything it can at you to get you to take notice. Do you remember the domains we talked about in skills group, how an emotion plays out in your body? *(T. reminds the client of the teaching of emotion regulation in skills group.)*

CLIENT: No… Oh, wait a minute. do you mean, facial expression and temperature and all that?

THERAPIST: Yes, those things are how the emotion tightens the screw around your guts, and biases your thinking so you CAN only see one side. If we do a little opposite action you might find it becomes easier to take a wise-mind position. If you are willing? I mean, I don't want to invalidate that the shame felt horrible. *(T. explains emotion theory and seeks an invitation to treat, remembering to validate the unpleas-antness of the emotion.)*

CLIENT: I couldn't have felt any worse, so I have nothing to lose. I was in the chair, just staring at the floor, but not really seeing it, you know? Just thinking, 'this is me, this is how people see me'.

THERAPIST: Show me how you were sitting *(client complies)* and I want you to act opposite to that position. Instead of slouch-ing, hold your muscles firm but not really tense, so it keeps your head up and your trunk more rigid. There's a reason we say, 'Hold your head up high' when we tell someone not to be ashamed. You can also drink some water to cool your-self down. So do it now in front of me. Relax your breath, not deep breathing, just your natural rate. *(T. activates be-havioural rehearsal.)*

CLIENT: *(Changes body posture, but continues to look down.)*

THERAPIST: Head up more. That's better. Sip your water. Now I wonder if last night your thoughts had a certain tone to them, I mean kind and gentle, harsh or critical, or somewhere be-tween? *(T. models how to attend to a different domain.)*

CLIENT: I was not being harsh to myself actually, I remember thinking, 'but care work is such a hard job, and I did it for years and years without complaining. People have no right to judge me'.

THERAPIST: *(Thoughtfully)* That's a helpful observation. Sounds like anger, but your body was slumped and your head down. I wonder, was it more like you were lashing out at those who might judge? Or like you were defending yourself in an argument? *(T. validates the client's observation, and invites curiosity.)*

CLIENT: Probably more defensive

THERAPIST: That makes sense, there's this dialectical effect that if you push hard on the door marked DEFENSIVE, it swings back and stamps 'GUILTY' on your forehead. So we need to keep the sentiments, but describe them more mindfully. *(T. uses a metaphor to describe a paradox – doing something that achieves the opposite of what you wanted.)*

CLIENT: I know what you mean, when I get defensive I always feel like I am on the losing side, which is ridiculous because I am only arguing with myself. That's so typical of me, even in an argument with myself I lose!

THERAPIST: *(Laughs)* On this occasion I will let that self-invalidation go, because your point is so good you might actually remember it next time you argue with yourself! *(T. makes an irreverent response about self-invalidation, because there is a higher learning point at stake.)* Imagine you're sitting in the chair and you notice this intense shame, your eyes and head drop, you feel hot, droop into the chair, and start to think about how people see you, becoming defensive in the process, now show me the opposite actions. *(T. activates behavioural rehearsal.)*

CLIENT: *(Changes her posture, holds her head up, relaxes her breathing)* I've forgotten what comes next.

THERAPIST: Why not take some notes? It is a lot to remember. *(T. encourages the problem-solving of obstacles.)*

CLIENT: OK, I've jotted down 'posture and breathing' and then…

THERAPIST: Sip your water for the temperature *(client complies)* and validate the bit of the emotion that fits the facts. Remember we were saying that some groups of people are judgemental. Just state it factually and confidently in a non-judgemental tone. *(T. gives clear instructions.)*

CLIENT: That's hard. *(Holds herself upright.)* OK… er… there are some people who would judge me for being on benefits. But they don't know my history.

THERAPIST: Lots of opposite actions there. You might want to say it again without the 'but'. Did it feel as intensely shameful as it did last night? *(T. invites curiosity about the effect of the skill.)*

CLIENT: When I said it, it still seemed defensive, like I was justifying because of my work.

THERAPIST: Good point. Why not reword it. *(T. encourages the client to rephrase until it touches her truth.)*

CLIENT: There are some people who would judge me for being on benefits, but there is always a background story.

THERAPIST: Great! it is almost impossible to feel quite as shameful if you are eliminating those shame signatures in your body and voice. I would just like you to change the 'but' to 'and at the same time' as that's more dialectical, maybe more specific about your history. Head up. *(T. gives corrective feedback.)*

CLIENT: *(More confidently.)* 'There are some people who will judge me for being on benefits, and at the same time, there is always a backstory to anyone on benefits'.

THERAPIST: Your tone was perfect there, I didn't hear any defensiveness. Did it feel like you were losing the argument? *(T. invites the client to assess how the skill is affecting their body experience of the emotion.)*

CLIENT: No. But I don't understand, I am saying pretty much the same thing as I did last night.

THERAPIST: The content of what you are saying is similar, but the 'how' is making a difference. We are breaking the cycle of behaving in a shameful way, which lowers the sensation of the emotion. Even saying, 'Some people' rather than 'everyone' will take the shame down a notch. *(T. gives a rationale for the opposite actions.)*

CLIENT: But you can't always tell who is making judgements about you, people don't say, they just think it.

THERAPIST: We're not the thought-police, so as long as people are not being rude or discriminatory, we can't hold their inner thoughts against them. I just wonder if in trying to predict what other people are thinking, you are influenced by your own thoughts about being on benefits? It's helpful to check out your opinions of yourself, in case they maintain shame. *(T. explores other controlling variables for shame.)*

CLIENT: Someone my age should be working, but I can't work, it's not that I haven't tried.

THERAPIST: Absolutely, so remember shame is all about hiding things. Here's my top tip – whatever makes you feel bad, if you can say it out loud, honestly and factually in a none-shameful way, it always feels better. Decide on a phrase that captures your thought, and avoid extremes. Try replacing 'Should be working' with 'I'd prefer to be working' and be kinder to yourself. If you can, remember your dialectics – use 'and' instead of 'but', and some reference to 'this moment'. *(T. encourages opposite action to shameful behaviour.)*

CLIENT: Er. 'I'd prefer to have work but... er, I mean 'and'... I am still unwell... right now'.

THERAPIST: That's better! Hold your head up, factual tone of voice, not rushed or defensive. Just a perfectly reasonable and honest statement. Say it again, then check out how it feels. *(T. coaches evaluation of the solution.)*

CLIENT: *(Head up, confident tone)* 'I'd rather be working, and right now I am still unwell'. That definitely feels different. Saying, 'I'd rather...' seemed to change it a lot.

THERAPIST: That's because you were using your own words instead of mine, and at the same time keeping to that middle ground. Your words, voice, and body language were signalling to your brain that it was not shameful. *(T. highlights the mechanism of change.)*

CLIENT: But do I just have to *accept* that people will judge me?

THERAPIST: Not at all! You always have the option to *deny* it... Denial is the opposite of acceptance. The main thing is not to confuse accepting that people judge, with accepting the content of their judgements. *(T. uses irreverence and makes a teaching point about judgements.)*

CLIENT: Huh, there's no point in denying it.

THERAPIST: I agree. And at the same time, for dialectical balance, we want to consider those who might be supportive. People who think in a similar way to you. Remember there's always more than one way to look at things. *(T. coaches more dialectics, looking for what is left out.)*

CLIENT: Even if the worst way to look at things has just been on the TV, right in front of you?

THERAPIST: Especially then. Acting opposite to shame also involves being 'loud and proud'. This is how minority groups have overcome stigma, by joining with others and forming campaigns. There are probably some political or charitable groups you can seek out that lobby for better treatment and less discrimination for those with mental health issues. These are your allies, and for the sake of better developed societies it is important for them to speak out. Not all views were represented by that documentary, and by acting opposite to hiding, things can change. Are you interested in any campaigns? *(T. explores all the avenues of opposite action.)*

CLIENT: Not really.

THERAPIST: ...and closer to home, do you have supportive friends or family? Professionals who help? Could you have made contact with them last night? That's another form of opposite action. Particularly is there anyone who would have shared your view? *(T. does not attach to any particular solution, just aims to present as many options for opposite actions.)*

CLIENT: People in skills group, probably. I don't know if they watched it.

THERAPIST: Not a bad idea. who would you call? *(T. pulls for behavioural specificity.)*

CLIENT: Lin, probably.

THERAPIST: And say? *(T. asks for more behavioural detail.)*

CLIENT: Did you see that documentary?

THERAPIST: Great! Now what have we learnt today? *(T. assesses how well the skill has been assimilated.)*

CLIENT: *(Reading from her notes.)* Shame doesn't make me a bad person, cool my body, get my head up, confident voice. Erm... accept some people will judge and that I don't always know. Find people who think more like me... say out loud what is on my mind, but not in an ashamed way, and the dialectics stuff – don't use extreme language about myself, say, 'rather' and all that. That was the best things, today, because I felt it being different. I think I got them all down.

THERAPIST: So if you could have done this on that day, would you have been more likely to want to harm yourself or less likely? *(T. checks the relationship between the solutions being rehearsed and the target behaviour.)*

CLIENT: I think... less likely... I actually *felt* different when I straightened up and spoke confidently. And I forgot to say that bit about shame telling you more about the group, it feels like a relief. I don't want to belong to those people.

Special considerations in regulating shame

1) Therapists and clients can fall into the trap of thinking that if shame ever turns up it is a disaster, rather than just one more in a whole symphony of emotions that are trying to help us. It can take some practice for therapists to master the art of treating shame like any other emotion, and model being matter of fact.

2) Shame is justified when risk of rejection is high. It is not necessarily a sign of wrongdoing. Here are some stories that can illustrate the point:

   a) An emotionally immature teen takes her beloved doll to school and is shamed by the reactions of her peers. The response of her fellow students lacks empathy and understanding, but the girl has done nothing wrong, she has behaved completely in line with her values. She still feels shame because she has been rejected by the group.

   b) In some social groups not having the most fashionable shoes or phone can lead to shame responses.

   c) We have terms such as 'body-shaming' or 'mum-shaming' referring to remarks made by a group (often online) about how you should look or how you should parent. These phrases acknowledge the social component of shame.

   d) If you hate tidying the house, and rarely do it, you might remain completely happy if you don't care about the untidiness and neither do your friends. And then you can flip into acute shame when someone new calls unexpectedly. The context always influences the outcome.

   e) Bridget Jones and the big pants. I rest my case.

3) When using mindful describing, as in the scenario above, the client needs to keep rewording his or her description until it accurately reflects the situation, checking in with themselves until it feels right. Speaking out loud is an opposite action for shame.

4) Much progress in human rights is owed to people refusing to be shamed by stigmatisation. Victims of 'shaming' who refuse to hide render the actions of their persecutors ineffective, and eventually they will cease.

5) Sometimes shame can be reduced to a feeling of guilt. For example if you promise to feed your friend's goldfish while she is on holiday, but forget and it dies, one option (shame) is to avoid your friend for the next ten years. Alternatively you could act opposite and ask what you can do to repair things. You still might risk rejection, depending on the amount of loss your friend suffered, and how much she blames you.

6) If the client has a legitimate reason to feel ashamed, it is unhelpful to reassure them or provide mitigation. For example, 'I feel ashamed because I caused a scene in the shop, pulling all the goods off the shelves and screaming when I was drunk'. Better to respond, 'Your shame was telling you that was a breach of social norms that could get you banned from the shop. I wonder what we can do to try and downgrade that to guilt, and maybe repair it?'

7) People who have been abused in childhood are often told to 'hide' the information, and that bad things will happen if they tell. This is a sure-fire way to seed shame in the victim. Often the child is removed from their home, thus reducing contact not only with the abuser but non-abusing members of their family, compounding their sense of being rejected. Revelations of sexual abuse to colleagues or friends can create more rejection if the listeners are ill-equipped to cope.

8) Feeling shame does not mean you are a bad person, in fact psychopaths often feel no shame. People who have well-developed consciences are more prone to guilt and shame.

When does shame need up-regulating?

If a client is showing nonchalance about behaving in ways that will foster rejection. For example, in an in-patient unit one resident had no qualms about spitting onto the dayroom carpet. This was upsetting to staff and other patients who would avoid the client (and the dayroom.) In another setting an adolescent girl would flash her breasts at the parents of other patients on the unit, particularly the fathers, and would be amused by their embarrassment. The aim of increasing shame is not to make the person feel bad, rather to act as a 'note to self' about the social consequences of undertaking this behaviour.

CHAPTER

12 | **Disgust**

When does disgust fit the facts?

Disgust fits the facts when there is a risk of contamination. In evolution this would have been an infection risk from expelled bodily fluids, such as blood, guts, sputum, vomit, and faeces. Disgust can also include social contamination, which is why we don't want to be around paedophiles.

In the disgust family: Contempt, revulsion, sick to the stomach, loathing, distaste, abhorrence, repugnance.

Action urges: To repel the cause of the disgust or recoil from it.

Function of the emotion: To protect from toxins or infection.

Signature features of disgust

* **Temperature:** Hot
* **Facial expression:** Head turned to the side, a distinctive lip curl on one side only, which probably blocked off one nostril when we had larger facial features. Eyes narrowed or closed to reduce contact with air-borne toxins

- **Breathing:** Breath-holding
- **Muscle tone:** Rigid, stomach clenching
- **Voice tone:** Silent, speechless, or a fragmented sneer, spitting the words out, to prevent an inhalation during speech
- **Posture:** A signature upper-body twist. This reduces the probability of ingesting airborne contaminants by twisting the mouth, nose, and eyes away, but prevents foot movements that might stir more toxins into the atmosphere. If we found ourselves in a contaminated area we would need to pick our way out slowly and carefully. This recoil posture probably gives rise to the expression 'giving someone the cold shoulder'.
- **Gesture:** Hand over the mouth, or hand up palm forward in a rejecting motion, along with the signature head turn, gagging or retching
- **Overt actions:** Avoiding the potential source of contamination.

Disgust example scenario

In the following example the client has cut her stomach after a social event with two female friends of the same age.

CLIENT: I just thought I deserved the pain, because those two have kept themselves in great shape, and when I looked at myself in the mirror, I looked disgusting. Rolls of fat around my waist, my dress was bulging over my belly. I am just revolting.

THERAPIST: Hmm, even as you say that now I can see your face is contorting at the memory, and your voice has adopted a sneering tone, is that how you looked and sounded that night? (*T. is awake to in-session behaviour and describes the signature features of disgust displayed by the client.*)

CLIENT: I didn't say anything out loud

THERAPIST: ...and did your thoughts have this kind of tone to them, sneering at yourself? *(T. asks about the internal tone the client is using towards herself.)*

CLIENT: I guess so, but it's true, I am revolting.

THERAPIST: It sounds like you are identifying the emotion as disgust? *(T. could have chosen a cognitive intervention, or mindfulness, to address the self-critical thought, but choose to work on reducing disgust. T. models a neutral voice in contrast to the client's judgemental tone.)* Do you remember from group when disgust fits the facts?

CLIENT: No... Er, wait, is it about poisons?

THERAPIST: Kind of, it's about contamination, stopping us from getting sick by ingesting something that would be bad for us. *(T. teaches about emotion function.)* So let's assess whether there was any risk of contamination here. *(T. pulls for behavioural rehearsal of checking the facts.)*

CLIENT: Not contamination, but *I felt* disgusted at the sight of myself.

THERAPIST: Then maybe we need to check out whether your friends displayed any disgust behaviours towards you, did they make unkind comments or seem to recoil from you? As that would increase the likelihood of you feeling 'disgusting'. Did they turn away, not want to sit with you or anything like that? *(T. takes the communication seriously, not moving too quickly to dispel disgust. T. models how to assess for the trigger factors that might have prompted the disgust.)*

CLIENT: No, they were really nice. It's more how I feel about myself.

THERAPIST: OK, so let's do another assessment for 'contamination'. Is there anything at all that could damage your health, or infect others. *(T. adopts a factual tone, and models how to check the facts.)*

CLIENT: It is unhealthy to be fat, and it you don't do something about it then you will just get bigger.

THERAPIST: OK, and do you think you were recoiling from your-self on health grounds, or more on how you appeared? *(T. continues to model checking the facts.)*

CLIENT: It wasn't on health grounds...

THERAPIST: Yeah, I agree, the disgust reaction seems out of pro-portion to the situation, there was no risk of toxins, and you went on to cut your stomach, which was harm in itself. *(T. describes the consequences factually.)*

CLIENT: But I hate looking like this.

THERAPIST: Hmm, we can't tell how much misery is being caused by your appearance, and how much by the revulsion you are directing towards yourself. By sneering and recoiling from your reflection you are stoking up those inner 'disgust' sensations. We might be able to get them down a bit. If you were willing? *(T seeks an invitation to treat.)*

CLIENT: But I deserve to feel this bad, look at me.

THERAPIST: *(Serious tone)* If we look strictly at the emotion, then there's no contamination risk so disgust is not valid. So I'm going to ask you a really important question, and I want you to be as honest as possible. Is there any evidence that if you ramp UP the amount of disgust you show to yourself, this will result in an improvement in your life? It just seems to me that you have tried directing revulsion at yourself and no good has come of it. But I will be guided by you. I am genuinely open to the idea I may be missing something? *(T. enquires about the consequences of maintaining this level of disgust.)*

CLIENT: *(Less confident in tone than when she was sneering at herself)* Er. That if I dropped the disgust maybe I would get fatter?

THERAPIST: The good news is that I'm not here to make your life worse, so if we try reducing the disgust and things de-teriorate for you we can always increase it again. My aim is to teach you to regulate emotion effectively. *(T. doesn't get drawn into a polarised position, but retains a dialectical stance.)*

CLIENT: It just doesn't feel OK to drop it.

THERAPIST: I can kind of understand that, almost as though you don't want to let yourself off the hook? Because of this idea you have let yourself go? I only say that because you mentioned that the other girls had kept in shape.

CLIENT: Exactly.

THERAPIST: Have you ever seen the episode of Fawlty Towers where Basil's car breaks down and he is so angry he breaks a branch off a tree and *beats* the car with it? I think everyone can relate to that level of anger, but the reason it's funny is because his actions are pointless, however justified he feels, beating the car is ridiculous. There's a parallel here with getting disgusted. You're not happy with something but the thing you are doing is not going to make it any better. *(T. uses an analogy to make the point about the emotion not serving a function in this case.)* We can always look at ways you can get in shape, if you want to.

CLIENT: I can't, I just fail.

THERAPIST: And it makes perfect sense that you turn on yourself at 11 o'clock at night, because you *can* get disgusted very easily at home alone in your bedroom, whereas you can't join a running group at that time, or start a new diet, or go swimming, or speak to a personal trainer. And even if you were to resolve to do them, all those things take a lot of guts when you feel so down about yourself. *(T. validates the difficulty of solving the problem, and shows how the emotion can be reinforced.)*

CLIENT: *(Gets tearful.)*

THERAPIST: *(Kindly)* And once you are the victim of such strong disgust, does it make it easier to get yourself to the gym? Or do you just feel more hopeless? *(T. validates the sense of hopelessness, linking it to the emotion.)*

CLIENT: More hopeless…

THERAPIST: *(Brightly)* Oh, and let's not forget telling yourself you deserve it… how's that working out for you? *(T. can risk being slightly irreverent, as the client's tears have relieved a little of the tension. This type of dialectical shift in style can be really helpful in activating behaviour in a critical point in the session.)*

CLIENT: *(Laughs)* OK, OK, I get the picture! So how can I get the disgust down?

THERAPIST: Let's go back to that night. Imagine you are in front of the mirror. I don't have a mirror here, so pretend this part of the wall is showing your reflection. Show me; how were you standing? Do the face…*(client pretends the wall is a mirror and complies).* OK, now see how you've turned your head slightly and narrowed your eyes? And you've kind of wrinkled your nose? I want you to keep your head straight forward, and not let yourself turn away. Shoulders square, good! Head up a little. Eyes more relaxed. Top lip down. That's better…. Oops, your head angled away just then, turn it back… *(T. elicits behavioural rehearsal and gives corrective feedback.)*

CLIENT: *(Complies with instructions.)*

THERAPIST: Just describe what you were seeing, and first let me hear your disgust voice – how you were saying it in your mind, on that day.

CLIENT: *(Sneering tone)* Look at my bulging stomach, ugh, it's disgusting, rolls of fat, ugh, I'm so ugly.

THERAPIST: OK, so what do you think you need to do? *(T. encourages the patient to describe the opposite actions.)*

CLIENT: Drop the sneer, lower my lip, use different words.

THERAPIST: Great! Just describe factually what you see… *(T. encourages behavioural rehearsal.)*

CLIENT: I see myself in a blue dress… er… I see… I'm wearing… er… silver earrings, those moon-shaped ones … and… I don't know… I'm more drawn to all the things I hate about myself.

THERAPIST: And those things will be there so we can describe them mindfully, such as, 'I see my dress curve over my stomach'. We don't want the pendulum to swing all the way from highlighting your least favourite bits to avoidance, because that wouldn't be dialectical, and avoidance tends to increase anxiety. Just leave out the judgements or criticisms. *(T. coaches a dialectical position.)*

CLIENT: I see my dress *curve* over my stomach...

THERAPIST: Whoa, stop there... you might have changed your words, but you are showing disgust with your tone and your face. Try again. And this time, move smoothly onto another observation, to balance it up. *(T. gives corrective feedback.)*

CLIENT: I see my dress curve over my stomach... and my silver earrings.

THERAPIST: You're doing great. *(T. cheerleads.)*

CLIENT: It's so hard... er... this is really... I have brown hair... my eyes are blue...

THERAPIST: Good job! What happened as you practised that? *(T. encourages evaluation.)*

CLIENT: My mind was just going crazy trying to hurl insults, all I could think of were those phrases I wasn't supposed to say.

THERAPIST: WELL DONE!! You didn't actually give in, and that forged some new neural networks as you rehearsed. It shows you don't have to be mean to yourself. And was the disgust higher or lower? *(T. gives a rationale for the new behaviour and checks the result on the emotion.)*

CLIENT: Lower.

THERAPIST: I'm going to own up to a fantasy I have, that if we just reduce the disgust everything is going to be OK. But that would be denying that that when you look in the mirror you are unhappy with what you see, and so we have to address that problem. Now, we have four ways to go with this; one is to get you in better shape.

CLIENT: I've done so much already, nothing's worked.

THERAPIST: OK, and we can add 'Being disgusted with myself' to that list of failed things, especially if they are activities you're not going to repeat. The good news is you don't have to do things you've tried before. We need to look for some new plans. Fortunately new ideas for getting in shape come out all the time, new exercise classes or new diets. Is it more that you don't have any ideas of what to do, or that they all take time to get results?

CLIENT: Yes, I want the results immediately. And because I don't get them I fall off the plan.

THERAPIST: That makes complete sense, we might have to use our acceptance skills on the amount of time it takes. Try saying to yourself, 'I want to change my appearance and I'd *prefer* if I could get results more quickly'. Say it out loud, in a non-disgusted voice. *(T. pulls for behavioural rehearsal of acknowledging the desire for a quick fix.)*

CLIENT: *(Complies)* Wow, that's weird.

THERAPIST: What?

CLIENT: Saying it out loud like that, it didn't seem nearly so bad.

THERAPIST: That's because saying, 'I'd prefer' is a very dialectical statement, it acknowledges both sides, wanting something and not necessarily getting it. What we say to ourselves really matters. So: Solution number two of four; we can also look at other ways to feel happier with your appearance, getting advice on styles and colours that flatter you, new hair and make-up. *(T. models assessing a range of solutions.)*

CLIENT: *(Shrugs)* I watch some of those make-up blogs already.

THERAPIST: And number 3, we can work on feeling better about yourself in ways that are not appearance-focussed; e.g. doing some climate-action work, becoming an age concern volunteer, knitting tiny bonnets for premature babies, walking dogs at the local Canine Care centre. Becoming a paramedic, visiting the pyramids, writing letters to young people in Africa who want pen-pals. Some of these things are really worthwhile and you don't even have to leave home to do them. The list is endless. It's a process of widening your vision beyond the thing you dislike about your appearance. *(T. encourages the expanding of perspectives.)*

CLIENT: So; get in shape, improve how I look in other ways, or find other things to like about myself, what's the fourth thing?

THERAPIST: It's accepting that you dislike how you look, allowing dislike to be there without letting it ruin your life. It's in the acceptance strategies that we did in group. Allowing an emotion to be there, without trying to fight it. Sometimes we have to sit with regret, at the same time knowing it's not the end of the world. *(T. includes an acceptance option to balance the change suggestions.)*

CLIENT: I want to fight it, though.

THERAPIST: Then we need to fight it effectively. I can help with any of these options, and I'm aware they might not feel appealing. So which of these might be the easiest, just as a starting point? *(T. gets alongside the client by validating the probable disillusionment before inviting her to make a choice.)*

CLIENT: *(Sighs)* Uh, maybe look at those other things apart from my appearance, that list of volunteering and stuff.

THERAPIST: We'd have to take it seriously, with proper research about what would suit your personality. Instead of being disgusted at yourself in the mirror, you need to see your reflection as someone who has come to you for advice, on how to shape up her life, not just her body. What would you do to help a friend at a crossroads in her life? *(T. demonstrates how the new behaviours are opposite to disgust and invites behavioural rehearsal.)*

CLIENT: Er, probably start looking up things she might like on the internet, and putting them in a folder for her on my laptop. I mean for me. I'm going to do it for me.

THERAPIST: Great, then get your laptop out and make the folder. And if you had done all these actions that are opposite to disgust on Friday – would you have been more likely or less likely to cut yourself? *(T. checks out the relationship between the skills rehearsed and the target behaviour.)*

CLIENT: I think it would be really hard to change, but at least I have options... where before it felt hopeless. I'd have to give it a go and see. But it's definitely different.

Special considerations in disgust

1) Where an emotion is clearly unjustified, if the therapist moves too quickly to dispel it, the client often assumes the therapist does not understand. Taking the disgust seriously is an essential part of teaching emotion regulation, otherwise it just becomes another way of telling a client they are wrong.

2) Tackling the source of disgust can be tricky if it involves the client's appearance, and therapists can avoid going 'where angels fear to tread'. But the message, 'this is too awful to mention' inadvertently reinforces the disgust. If the client was in perfect shape and still felt disgusted, the therapist might have said, *'Once you have achieved the healthy norms for weight, if your disgust is still present, I think we need to look elsewhere to make the change'*.

3) If you act opposite to disgust it comes down very quickly. A nurse once told me that in her training on the physical health wards the matron told the new recruits, 'You must NEVER exhibit disgust when handling a bed pan, or dressing a wound, as it is totally unprofessional'. Within a couple of weeks neither she nor her co-students felt any disgust during those tasks. Such is the power of opposite action.

4) A mini-version of the signature lip curl is the 'dimpler flash' – so called because it is a result of contracting the dimpler muscle between the upper lip and left nostril. This

has been identified by relationship therapist John Gottman et al. (2001) as a marker of interpersonal contempt. He and his team noted that by counting the number of dimpler flashes in a 15-minute segment of marital therapy, they could reliably predict which couples were going to divorce rather than reconcile. Furthermore, being on the receiving end of a dimpler flash increased the recipient's heart rate by an average of two beats per minute. It's the equivalent of a psychological slap.

5) Disgust in therapy is most commonly seen in relation to the following presentations:

- Eating disorders, where people may experience disgust at either perfectly healthy food, or at their own body
- Body dysmorphia
- Phobias (check out in a spider phobia if it is fear or disgust the person feels)
- OCD.

There are evidence-based protocols for addressing these problems and the therapist should use these when appropriate. However, where disgust just crops up as a link in the chain to self-harming behaviour (as in this scenario) it can be very useful to employ an opposite action.

6) Being considered 'untouchable' can elicit feelings of disgust towards the self. We need to be aware of how often self-harm behaviours function to elicit touch from others. Clients in contained environments often only get touched during a course of treatment, or by provoking restraint. When either shame or disgust flare repeatedly, check out if the client's 'being touched' levels are low. Some institutions have introduced hand massages to counter this problem.

7) The signature turn of the head and upper body are so powerful in disgust, yet is often underestimated by the therapist.

I encourage you to get the client to face the object of their disgust square on, relaxed shoulders, face forward, without turning away. The effect will surprise you both.

When does disgust need up-regulating?

It doesn't happen often, but sometimes clients engage in particularly disgusting behaviour (such as eating scabs) and describe how the physiology can be addictive (e.g. heart racing, an adrenaline buzz, a sense of defiance). If such behaviour crops up in a chain analysis it is useful to look at what other emotions (or thoughts) go away when disgust arises, and at alternative methods of getting an adrenaline high or rebelling. The aspects of the disgust that are missing are recoiling, narrowing the eyes, repelling the substance, and gagging. These can be rehearsed in imagination, in association with the undesirable behaviour.

Reference

Gottman, J., Levenson, R., & Woodin, E. (2001). Facial expressions during marital conflict. *Journal of Family Communication, 1*(1), 37–57.

13 Envy and jealousy

When do envy and jealousy fit the facts?

Jealousy and **envy** might be considered 'mirror emotions', which is why the terms are often confused.

Envy fits the facts when someone else has something you want. It might be a relationship, a possession, status, or talent.

Action urges for envy: To reduce the discrepancy between you and the envied person

1) By gaining the same thing – e.g. copying their haircut or buying the same car.

2) By destroying the thing they have, either by physically taking it away or destroying the pleasure they might get from it – e.g. sneering at their taste, or highlighting faults with whatever it is they value.

Function of Envy: In evolution envy may have provided motivation to improve our circumstances by viewing and attaining what others have, and also to keep the stability of a group as people tend to gravitate towards those with similar standards. If discrepancies can be kept to a minimum the group is less likely to fragment. Puncturing the ego of someone who is pulling ahead might prevent one person dominating a group.

Emotion families: Envy might be considered refrigerated anger, feeling blocked and an urge to attack, but with the heat taken out of it. Probably because to act quickly would give the game away. In the envy family: Greedy, covetous, grasping, yearning, competitive.

Signature features of envy

These are very muted, as envy and jealousy are not socially acceptable. We strive particularly hard to keep envy from our face, body, and voice, as to allow someone to know they are envied would hand them an even bigger social advantage.

- **Temperature:** Cool or cold
- **Facial expression:** Thin-lipped, Brows slightly lowered. Unresponsive in expression
- **Breathing:** Controlled
- **Muscle tone:** Tense, trying not to give away signs of the emotion.
- **Voice tone:** Inhibited speech
- **Posture:** Rigid
- **Gesture:** Minimal or dismissive
- **Overt actions:** Copying, or trying to replicate what the envied person has. Destroying the other person's advantage, or spoiling it. Making put-down remarks about what is envied to reduce or eliminate the owner's pleasure. Someone who

has envy might even criticise something that they actually like or admire. This hostility can seep into other aspects of the relationship. For example, famous actors describe how in addition to accolades from fans they also get trolled on social media or people pick fights with them. Giving rise to the phrase, 'taking down a peg or two'.

Jealousy fits the facts when we risk losing something precious to another person. It could be a relationship, an object, status, or reputation.

Action urges of jealousy: To jealously guard what we value, and keep other people at a distance from taking it. To prevent others equalling our achievements.

Function of jealousy: To preserve an advantage. In evolution having higher status in the group might have conferred protection and therefore increased longevity.

Families of emotions: Jealousy might be considered part of the **fear** family – having at its heart anxiety about potential loss. In the jealousy family: Selfish, protective, mean.

Signature features of jealousy

- Temperature: Heated
- Facial expression: Scowling, glaring, warning off the threat
- Breathing: A slight hold on the inbreath, but not noticeably so (preparing for defensive action if needed)
- Muscle tone: Tense
- Voice tone: Firm
- Posture: Rigid
- Gesture: Height-increasing, e.g. stretching the neck, raising the head, as if the physical presence will ward off the threat

- Overt actions: Preventing anyone taking or replicating your success. Hiding valuables, warning people away. Positioning yourself protectively between what you value and any potential threats. In a relationship, checking up on a partner, reading their messages, timing their journeys, and controlling their actions and what they wear, so as to reduce the likelihood that they will stray.

Jealousy example scenario

I have chosen to focus on jealousy, as this causes more clinical problems than envy. In the following example the client's target behaviour is an urge to take an overdose after his girlfriend, Shona, threatened to leave, accusing him of 'being a control freak'.

THERAPIST: Ah, so has she left already? *(T. assesses consequences of the behaviour.)*

CLIENT: No, but I feel like we're hanging on by a thread. I wish I could stop being jealous, but, you know, she was with someone else when we started dating. And she is really beautiful. I know she cares about me but I'm driving her away. I can't help myself.

THERAPIST: OK, that sounds upsetting. Let's look at Friday, when you had the row, what was happening in your body? *(T. validates and draws attention to the physiology of the emotion.)*

CLIENT: I saw her getting ready for her colleague's leaving party. I'd offered to drop her off but her friend Sunita was picking her up. I was cool with it, but then she looked amazing, and so happy. I just felt my guts clenching, I walked away because it made it worse watching her.

THERAPIST: When you noticed your stomach tightening, did you remember what we did in group about opposite action?

What would that have involved? *(T. reminds the client of the skill and invites behavioural rehearsal.)*

CLIENT: *(Doubtful tone)* Yeah, I remember that stuff about relaxing my muscles, but... *(fidgets)* I don't know who was going to be at the dinner with her. We met at an office party when she was with her previous partner, so I'm not being irrational.

THERAPIST: Ah, yes, so it makes perfect sense that you had associations with past incidents. And does that give rise to the anxiety? *(T. offers some validation and enquires more about the emotion.)*

CLIENT: Exactly, like if I drop my guard she'll be off.

THERAPIST: You've hit the nail on the head there, about guarding, that's exactly what jealousy motivates us to do. So if we look at what happened on Friday, did the stomach clenching lead to any other 'guarding' behaviours? *(T. explains the function of the emotion, and encourages the client to be mindful of other similar actions.)*

CLIENT: I was looking out of the window, checking to make sure it was Sunita coming for her and not some stud.

THERAPIST: OK, I can follow the logic in that, if you were fearful of her running off with someone. Could you just rephrase, 'some stud' as that's going to make you more anxious. *(T. encourages behavioural rehearsal of mindful describing.)*

CLIENT: You know, a man, someone I don't know, who might be attractive to Shona.

THERAPIST: And I do understand that this was your fear. Let's just get a list of the behaviours, anything else? *(T. validates the emotion so that the client will not feel ashamed of the revelations, and stays matter of fact about behaviour.)*

CLIENT: Then I had a quick look at her phone. I don't usually do that.

THERAPIST: OK... *(T. gives the client opportunity to review the statement without directly challenging.)*

CLIENT: Well, I haven't done it for a while

THERAPIST: Anything else? Anything internal to you? *(T. expands the client's observation to the internal cues.)*

CLIENT: I was quite hot by this point, and pacing a bit.

THERAPIST: If I'd seen your face, what would I have seen *(T. draws attention to facial expression.)*

CLIENT: She said I had 'a face like thunder'

THERAPIST: Ah, you were obviously feeling some strong unpleasant emotion at that point, and the facial expression had a knock-on effect with Shona? *(T. validates both sides of the dialectic – that he was having a hard time as well as his partner.)*

CLIENT: I felt completely chewed up inside. And then I ended up sitting up in the front room till the early hours of the morning waiting for her to come back. When she got in I gave her a grilling; I just wanted to know who she sat with and what they talked about. She'd been drinking, so it just ended up as a screaming row.

THERAPIST: Oh no, pretty awful for both of you then... and yet at some level this jealousy is working for you, because all the actions you took help you to feel like you are guarding this relationship, they're a kind of safety behaviour. Getting rid of them would have a cost, and I'm not here to make your life worse. *(T. plays devil's advocate, taking the position of keeping things as they are. This is useful if the client might feel threatened by change, or resist.)*

CLIENT: You can't make it worse, she's threatening to leave me.

THERAPIST: What I mean is, letting go of those behaviours is going to cause you a lot of anxiety. Right now the fear of her leaving is worse, but if she decides to stay you would lose that motivation. And you wouldn't be able to go back to being jealous again. *(T. clarifies the contingencies around changing the behaviour.)*

CLIENT: *(Winces)* I don't have a choice, though, do I?

THERAPIST: *(Calmly)* You do. You can decide this relationship is too distressing, or not worth the anxiety. We don't have to be with anyone if we don't want to be. I don't just want to keep you on the merry-go-round. *(T. highlights what the client is missing out, that there are choices, even if they are unpleasant. T also seeks an invitation to treat.)*

CLIENT: I want to be less jealous, it has come up in other relationships, I can't keep doing this.

THERAPIST: Well first we need to see if the jealousy is valid. Do you remember the teaching from group? *(T. pulls for the skill.)*

CLIENT: When you're scared someone might want to take what you have...

THERAPIST: Not quite, that's how it *feels*, but it's really when there is a genuine risk someone is trying to take something that belongs to you. *(T. clarifies when the emotion fits the facts.)*

CLIENT: That's exactly what I'm worried about, that someone will try and take her away from me.

THERAPIST: Can I ask, is it more the loss of her you worry about? Or losing out to someone else? *(T. checks the function of the behaviour.)*

CLIENT: Both, it would be awful to think of losing her and that she would be with another man. But. I'm not stupid, I know I'm pushing her away. I just can't help it. I see her phone and I just have this irresistible urge to pick it up.

THERAPIST: It's because 'emotions love themselves' so when you get jealous it drives multiple guarding behaviours, even if they don't work to strengthen the bond between you and your girlfriend. And is there anyone at work you particularly worry is making a play for Shona? *(T. validates and avoids saying, 'do you have any evidence?' Because that phrase can be interpreted as, 'you don't have any evidence, do you?' T. keeps a conversational style.)*

CLIENT: I suspect everyone, but nobody has marked themselves out.

THERAPIST: Right. Well this is a difficult emotion to regulate because relationship jealousy is a throwback to when there was a lot more coercion involved in coupling up. In most modern societies we prefer to choose partners freely. But jealousy tricks us into thinking we can prevent free will by limiting the possibilities to exercise it. Jealousy says if you stop Shona making calls, going out, and sitting with guys at dinner she will stay with you, not because she wants to, but because there's no opportunity to stray. *(T. describes the function of the emotion.)*

CLIENT: I don't want her to stay for that reason, it makes me sound desperate. But then I must be desperate because I think, honestly, I would take that reason as long as it means she doesn't leave… Maybe. I don't know… I suppose I'd be angry because I'd know deep down she wasn't really choosing to be with me.

THERAPIST: Perfectly understandable. So is it at all possible to capture a dialectic on this? A phrase you can say to yourself that sums up those conflicting emotions? Use your wise mind and find something that feels like it touches your own truth. *(T. validates, then encourages a dialectical position.)*

CLIENT: *(Sighs… pauses)* I… I feel really sad at the thought of losing her, and at the same time I want her to stay because she's choosing to be with me. *(Pause)* It's hard to believe she *would* choose me, though.

THERAPIST: I think you've hit the nail on the head, there, jealousy runs rampant if we don't think we'd be picked through free will. So you have to check the facts, not only about whether Shona is in the business of seeking a new mate, but if she found one, whether you'd prefer to restrain her from leaving you? *(T. encourages the client to check the facts.)*

CLIENT: *(Sighs… pauses)* I don't think there is anyone. And if there was… *(sighs… long pause)*.

THERAPIST: *(Lightly)* We can always keep the restraining version! *(T. gives ample time for reflection and then balances the conversation with an irreverent remark. This is a dialectical strategy to inhibit the client's mood from dropping too low. There is evidence with the sighing that the client is connecting with the sadness.)*

CLIENT: *(Hollow laugh)* It's not worked so far. I was just having to face the consequences of allowing her to go if she wants to.

THERAPIST: *(Seriously)* Break-ups are painful, and in some weird paradoxical twist, we are having to contemplate allowing her to leave, freely, in order to increase the chances that she might stay. If we could drop the checking behaviours the bond between you might strengthen, although we can't guarantee it. *(T. loses the irreverence as the client has not matched that, and highlights the paradox, which is another dialectical strategy.)*

CLIENT: What does it involve?

THERAPIST: In your dialectical statement you can own the sadness of losing her, but it's harder to think of letting her go, and I think that's maybe to do with feeling defeated by the sadness. So we want to give you a little confidence that you would cope. You told me you didn't want to sound desperate, so this time, hold your posture with dignity, keep your head up, and raise your eyebrows a tiny bit. Breathe evenly.... OK, your shoulders are creeping up a bit fearfully so keep them level... yes, that's better. Now say your statement again, with a more confident tone. *(T. coaches actions opposite to sadness.)*

CLIENT: I will be sad at losing her, and at the same time, I want her to stay because she wants to and not because I am forcing her to.

THERAPIST: Did that feel any different? *(T. gets feedback from the client on the effectiveness of the skill.)*

CLIENT: It did, actually, not great, but not as painful.

THERAPIST: Well, a little relief comes from allowing yourself to experience sadness without fighting it. We don't have to mourn her, because she hasn't gone, but we do have to have a sense that we could survive it. Remember your brain is reading your body. Now what's the opposite of 'guarding' behaviour? *(T. gives a rationale for regulating emotion.)*

CLIENT: Being generous, but what would that mean in a relationship? I'm not going to suggest she sleeps around!

THERAPIST: It's more about generosity of spirit. Jealousy is paranoid, and gets you acting like people are trying to steal from you, whereas generosity of spirit is kinder to people, and kinder about them, too. It would mean saying to Shona, 'Why not have a night out with your friends?' And resisting the urge to check her phone or grill her, acting as if you had trust in her. Not because this will stop her leaving, but because it is a less painful way to live your life. It still allows you to be sad about losses, but you don't have to experience them every day in your imagination. *(T. gives the rationale for acting opposite to jealousy.)*

CLIENT: This is going to be really hard.

THERAPIST: Which is why you don't have to do it. But if you *want* to do it, what's your next step? *(T. goes to the other side of the dialectic to highlight the principle of 'freedom to choose', which is particularly valuable in treating jealousy. Also pulls for behavioural rehearsal.)*

CLIENT: I knew all along I have to stop checking on her. But I didn't know those physical things would make it easier. I have to test it out when I'm with her. I'm not convinced. I mean, it was easier here with you, but with her, I can't help myself.

THERAPIST: When you notice that thought, 'I can't help myself' does make it easier or harder to try? What can you say to yourself instead? *(T. troubleshoots the obstacle.)*

CLIENT: Harder. I feel like you want me to do that dialectical business, or mindfulness or whatever, but actually I *liked* that 'generosity of spirit' idea. I can see that I haven't had that, not when it comes to the relationship, anyway. But I need any points I can get. I think she'd be really shocked, in a good way. It would drive me nuts to do it, but it makes a lot of sense.

THERAPIST: You got me completely right on 'dialectics' – I am a fan! But whatever works for you is more important, I will always be guided by you. So let's track the behaviours you want to change on the diary card, and we can see how it goes during the week. (*T. Models flexible responding, allowing people to choose their own path, which is the skill the client needs in the relationship.*)

Special considerations in regulating jealousy and envy

- In my clinical observations I have found that clients rarely discuss either envy or jealousy without also demonstrating aspects of other emotions. In the scenario above the client has both fear of losing his girlfriend, and when he allows himself to contemplate it, an overwhelming sadness.

- Envy often crops up in chains of bullying behaviour amongst teenagers, particularly girls. A typical phrase would be, 'I wanted to wipe that smile off her face because she thinks she's so amazing'. In many cases the girl that is envied may not seem (to the therapist) to be provocative, but does have attractive features or talents. Envy in these circumstances might be a form of competitive attractiveness and function to reduce the power of one's rivals in the dating stakes.

- Opposite actions to envy are paying compliments to the envied person, resisting the urge to puncture their joy, inhibiting gossiping about them, including rather than excluding them from activities, and, as in the case of jealousy, allowing them the advantage rather than competing.

- Jealousy has been a driving force for many crimes of passion, including most distressingly the murder of children to prevent an estranged spouse from having them (often followed by the suicide of the murderer). It shows just how strong this emotion can be. It is always worth checking out if there are any action urges of violence or malicious damage.

- I have found clients quite like the idea of generosity of spirit because most people prefer to be thought of as generous, and it is the opposite of being defeated or having someone 'get one over' on you. It can bestow a lift in self-esteem where this is low.

When do jealousy and envy need up-regulating?

Rarely so an exception might be in evoking envy as a motivator to more functional behaviour. For example, if a teenager is not doing any revision for exams, it might help to imagine his or her friends going off to Uni and having a great time. However this would only be functional if the required behaviour – revising, passing, and getting to university – is well within the adolescent's capability; otherwise, it can lead to despair. I would recommend only using this strategy if the adolescent is *asking* for help with motivation, and not as a stick to beat them with for failure to study.

14 Secondary emotions and contingencies

What are secondary emotions?

Secondary emotions are those that arise as a response to the primary emotion, such as

1) Feeling afraid of being sad – sadness is primary then fear takes over. This might happen if in the past sadness has led to unbearable pain. As fear rises the sadness diminishes.

2) Feeling ashamed of being angry – anger is primary then shame bubbles up. An example is when someone who is normally quite controlled loses their temper, seeing themselves in that state may elicit shame. At which point the anger will go down.

3) Feeling disgusted at being happy – happiness is the first emotion and then disgust comes to the fore. An example is someone who 20 years ago was convicted of causing death by dangerous driving. Any happiness quickly turns into disgust, 'how dare I enjoy this when I have taken someone else's life?'

There is not always such an obvious link between primary and secondary emotions. Sometimes the shift is due to a preference for the sensations caused by one emotion over another.

1) When the person feels guilty they get angry – anger just feels much more bearable than guilt.

2) When the person feels angry they start crying – tears of sadness feel more tolerable than feeling pumped up with anger.

3) When a person feels anxious they start laughing. It's not necessarily that they feel joyous, but the laughter – a signature feature of joy – makes the anxiety easier to bear.

In each of these examples the client may move so quickly to the secondary emotion that the primary emotion is unnoticeable. The only indication to the therapist is that the emotion on display doesn't seem a good fit for the situation. Therapists get very tied up in trying to identify what is primary and what is secondary, so it is helpful to revisit some basic principles about emotions and revise the main points from previous chapters.

- A person may only experience one emotion at once. (Remember the exercise from Chapter 2 of asking people to show the facial expression that goes with being heartbrokenly sad and at the same time furiously angry.)

- It is possible to move very quickly from one emotion to another, or to cycle rapidly through a series of emotions, which sometimes gives the *impression* of experiencing lots of emotions at once. It is more mindful to describe this as 'having a number of emotions over the course of a few seconds'.

- Events, thoughts, and emotions have an effect on what comes after them. Nothing happens in a vacuum. Whatever happens within the course of an emotional episode will affect its trajectory. If you start crying and the family dog jumps on your lap, the outcome will be different depending on whether you are comforted by the dog, or notice it is very smelly.

- When people say they feel an emotion all the time (e.g. 'I am always sad' or 'My shame never goes away'), this means that the neural architecture for one emotion fires up very quickly in comparison to others. This rapid-firing can give the *impression* that someone is feeling an emotion constantly. In reality it comes and goes.

- Most emotions, like anxiety and anger are hugely calorific, it is impossible to maintain them permanently.

- An emotion that is not re-started (by revisiting the trigger that set it off) will subside very quickly. So if you encounter a cue that elicits sadness, it will rise and fall within a few minutes. It is your interpretations that prolong the experience (Verduyn et al. 2011).

- Distracting from an emotion can reduce the intensity of it very quickly, but will be more likely to increase the response intensity the next time the person encounters that same cue (Thiruchselvam et al. 2011).

- The only emotion that it is possible to regulate is the one the person is currently having. Therefore even if you suspect this is secondary to a different emotion, you need to regulate the obvious one first.

So during supervision if a therapist tells me, 'I think this emotion of anger was a secondary emotion,' I say, 'Don't worry about it, regulate that, and if it is secondary, then as it reduces you will notice that the primary emotion will surface'.

Here is an example in which a client has lost her good friend following an argument, but only describes feeling anger. The therapist suspects this is secondary to sadness, but sticks with the principles of working on what's obvious rather than going on a fishing expedition.

THERAPIST: So after your friend left your house, and just before you banged your head, what was the emotion? *(T. focusses on the emotion link in the chain.)*

CLIENT: I was just livid, I mean, all the things she had accused me of, it was ridiculous. Good riddance, I say. I am so much better off without her. I know I asked her to stay, but I shouldn't have begged like that, because I do not miss her at all. Not one bit. It is her loss. And she walked off anyway, so, that was that. My anger was so strong, I ended up banging my head on the wall to get rid of it. It was so annoying.

THERAPIST: OK, let's look at the part of the emotion that was valid – nobody likes to be accused of things they haven't done. That would certainly constitute a threat. And you were blocked from giving your side? *(T. validates where anger might fit the facts.)*

CLIENT: Yes, I'm not saying I was completely innocent, but she brought up things from years ago.

THERAPIST: Oh no, how annoying, everyone hates that. And she isn't up for hearing you out? Maybe not at the time, but if you asked to meet up now, maybe? *(T. suggests problem-solving for the part of the emotion that would be valid.)*

CLIENT: There's no way. She just doesn't want to see me.

THERAPIST: And were you aware of that at the time? That she didn't want to see you? *(T. takes the client back to discussing the incident.)*

CLIENT: Yes, it was very final, when she turned...

THERAPIST: Right, and the anger flashed up immediately? *(T. doesn't suggest the client might have been sad at this point, but asks the client for her own observations, coaching emotional literacy.)*

CLIENT: She just gave me NO CHANCE to defend myself, it was a done deal, she just said her bit and flounced off. It's outrageous.

THERAPIST: OK, you obviously still feel angry now, so maybe we could get it down a bit, so that it is not so annoying for you. *(T. validates the anger.)* I think I could help. Do you remember the opposite actions to anger? Let's imagine we're back in that moment and she's just left. Sit or stand exactly how you did on the day, and notice what you feel like doing? *(T. elicits the action urge.)*

CLIENT: Following her...

THERAPIST: Do you think that would have helped? You know her best so I'll be guided by you on that. *(T. treads carefully, allowing the client time to work this out for herself. Following can be a sign of sadness, e.g. recovering what is lost, or of anger, e.g. following to attack.)*

CLIENT: No, I don't think so.

THERAPIST: OK, let's do some opposite action to anger – maybe turning and walking the other way, and remember how to smooth out any frown lines on your forehead, with your hand if necessary. Do it now so I can see. *(T. coaches opposite action to anger in a couple of domains, 'actions in the environment' and 'facial expression'.)*

CLIENT: *(Begins turning, runs her hand over forehead.)* She is just out of order. *(Sounds less dogmatic.)*

THERAPIST: When those thoughts come through your mind, focus on a nice long outbreath, and drop your shoulders, loosen your hands. *(T. coaches more opposite actions to anger.)*

CLIENT: *(Ignores the instructions, frowning.)* It's good riddance, you know. I'm not going to miss her. She will miss me more. I'm not bothered. *(This often happens when reducing a secondary emotion, the client begins to feel the primary, and tenses up again, rekindling the protective emotion of anger.)*

THERAPIST: *(Continues coaching)* Just loosen your jaw, walk more slowly, maybe find a place to sit, over here… that's it, shoulders down, good! Focus on that out-breath – nice… OK, your face just fell, what happened there? *(T. is awake to a change in the client's presentation that doesn't fit the emotion of anger.)*

CLIENT: I don't know, I just… You know… It's not because of her, it's just painful *(has a catch in the voice more appropriate to sadness than anger).*

THERAPIST: Of course it is, you have suffered a loss, even if the friendship was not great. Anyone would find that hard. You used to do a lot together… I'm thinking maybe it's sadness that you are feeling in this moment, but I could be wrong, it could be the pain of feeling annoyed. *(T. validates the pain and encourages the climate to name the emotion.)*

CLIENT: *(Tearfully)* Yes… *(pause…)* we go back a long way… I… I hate feeling sad.

THERAPIST: That makes complete sense. It's a very painful emotion. I wonder…when you feel angry does that sadness go away? Anger can flare up as a kind of protective factor. We could look out for that. *(T. validates the primary emotion and teaches emotional literacy by highlighting the sequencing and potential function of the emotions.)*

It is important to remember that secondary emotions are normal. The client is not lying or faking the anger, they genuinely feel it, and when they do, the sadness is not present. Humans have preferences for some emotions over others. If they can plot the easiest path through a challenging situation they will. Have you ever asked a colleague or family member about something they promised to do but forgot? Have they ever become cross with you for asking? In that instance crossness feels more comfortable for them than guilt.

If you are fairly sure the client is presenting a secondary emotion, you might wonder if paying attention to it is colluding with the client's avoidance. So in the case above, instead of faffing around trying to regulate the anger, why not confront the client with the evidence of the loss and go straight to a statement like, 'it seems like you're not friends any more, and I guess you will miss her?' This would be ignoring the anger and validating the emotion of sadness. I would suggest that the therapist has a choice between choosing an exposure technique, where the main aim is to get the client to *feel* the primary emotion, versus enhancing emotional literacy, where the goal is to *educate* the client in the complex relationships between emotions.

Personally, if the client is completely emotion-phobic and I get relatively few chances to present a cue for sadness, I might go for blocking the anger and just trying to elicit sadness, as exposure. But mostly I would prefer to coach the client to work through these steps for herself, so she can understand; *sometimes when I start to regulate an emotion I find a different one comes up, so I needn't be surprised when that happens. Emotions are complicated.* We hopefully land in the same place anyway – with the client experiencing the primary emotion.

Contingencies surrounding emotion regulation

Secondary emotions are an example of internal contingencies (meaning consequences that are experienced inside the client's body). The effect of them is to create a glitch in the system, so that the emotional experience is more complicated than usual. Environmental factors that can have the same effect, so that an emotion's presentation and the regulation of it are not straightforward. The following list describes confounding factors that can derail attempts to regulate emotion.

- **Cultural influences:** It is more acceptable to show emotion in some cultures than in others. A mild display of anger in

Brazil may appear as raging fury in Scandinavia, although this is also an example of racial stereotyping so cannot be assumed. Better for the therapist to be aware of cultural issues and still assess the effect. Gender identity also affects emotionality with messages like 'men don't cry'. One client told me his fear of showing emotion was receding, but unless all his macho colleagues had therapy too it would be an uphill struggle at work.

- **Status considerations:** People express emotion differently depending on whether they are speaking to a spouse, a psychiatrist, a child in their care, a neighbour, a job interviewer, or their closest friend. And the same status-role that is inhibitory for some is inflammatory for others. For example, a police officer's arrival can instantly deflate a houseful of partying 18-year-olds, yet inflame a domestic abuse incident if one party believes they have been reported to the law.

- **Loss of service provision:** Some clients fear that regulating emotion will make their life worse. They might lose benefits, or be discharged from services. Here's a common example; An in-patient unit provides a sense of security. But as soon as clients are deemed 'better' they are transferred or sent home, losing the lifeline that has contributed to their recovery. Clients also describe how their emotional pain is taken less seriously once they are more moderate in their communication (Dunkley et al. 2018).

- **Relationship changes:** Clients may lose important relationships as they change how they handle emotion. A mother once told me, 'I've been too emotionally unstable to care for the children, so my partner has had to do it. As soon as I am better, I know it, he'll be off. He's stayed because the kids need him'. It was an important factor for us to consider, and in fact he did leave just as she had predicted.

- **Organisational constraints.** Here's an example: An adolescent repeatedly reported feeling sad that her Mum and Dad seemed not to care for her. Her therapist said, 'Her parents never come to meetings or bring her to appointments. They don't visit when she's an in-patient. They rarely return her calls or ours. But I could never say that to her, they'd raise a complaint'. The girl's legitimate emotion escalated in the face of this invalidation, as she tried harder and harder to get someone to listen.

There is another factor that we sometimes overlook. People are such emotional beings that we pay the highest wages in society not to our heart surgeons or our political leaders, but to those who manipulate our emotions in film and sport. The people who give us our emotional highs command the top whack. At the other end of the scale, when we experience the least emotion is when we are in a deep coma or dead. Flat-lining emotionally is as terrifying as losing control. This threat can make the innocuous invitation to regulate an emotion sound to the client like this:

> Work with me and I can help you establish long periods in which nothing at all will happen. No drama, no lows or highs. You will not be the focus of attention, speculation or intense care. In fact you will hardly be noticed.

For some this might be a blessed relief from emotional torment, but for others this prospect *is* emotional torment. Those particularly at risk of boredom-phobia are those without work or social connections. This is not just true for patients. A colleague of mine attended one of my lectures and said afterwards, 'Now I know why when I'm between relationships I take on madcap projects. I'm craving that emotional intensity'. We all need to have the full symphony of emotions, even the low notes.

Here is an example from my own life. When I was a stay-at-home mum with my firstborn I had a recurring experience. I would be washing-up or putting away the laundry and think, 'I love my baby SO much, how does anyone cope with the loss of a child?' I would imagine how awful it would be if my baby was sick, and then if nothing could be done, to face the unthinkable loss... I could picture the faces of the doctors telling me the bad news, and before long I would be weeping into my clean tea-towels. At the time, as a trainee clinician I was in counselling myself, and my therapist told me, 'This is a fear-fantasy, you are bored, you need to get back to work'. I was highly indignant, but taking her advice I resumed my employment and the fear-fantasies stopped. My caseload provided me with plenty of emotional stimulation and the days I had at home with my daughter could be thoroughly enjoyed without any self-induced drama. To be clear, I am definitely NOT saying that emotional incidents are 'attention-seeking', but I am pointing out the dialectic – that not enough emotion over a period of time can be as bad as too much.

I taught this recently in an emotion regulation workshop and a delegate commented,

> I always get accused of sabotaging my own happiness. Just when everything seems settled I want to change jobs or move house. But actually I think I fear everything becoming really run of the mill. When you described this need for emotional variety it made complete sense.

And it's not just about excitement. I once watched the very sad film *Steel Magnolias* with my friend while our partners went to the pub. On their return we were sobbing uncontrollably. 'Ah, enjoying this then?' was my husband's retort. And the amazing thing was, yes, we were! We *need* emotion intensity, and if it is not happening naturally in our environment we will create it.

Summary

We cannot end without returning to our 'forest and trees' analogy. The whole philosophy behind DBT is that emotions are not a problem in themselves, but alert us to problems, and if we listen to them we can live a more authentic life. By teaching emotion regulation, we are helping clients to tend those emotional trees. But that's not enough. We also need our emotions to give us a sense of direction. If we are treating a client using these strategies and things are not improving, we can suspect that there might be a gaping hole in their life that the emotion is repeatedly flagging up. The old adage, 'Somewhere to live, someone to love, something to do' is a useful reminder of universal drivers:

- Does the person have adequate security in their accommodation? Being in substandard housing, having an uncertain tenancy, or just living too far from family and friends can take their toll. In-patients need to feel familiar with their onward accommodation before they will be ready to leave their current location.

- Does the client have rewarding structured activities? It's a dialectic; poor employment or high-pressure jobs make people worse, and so do huge swathes of unstructured time. The lifeline of benefits can become a tether, making clients feel guilty about enjoying life. People thrive with a sense of purpose and belonging, so a charitable cause, an education class, or a work team provides extra relational security. However, feeling pushed into employment can destroy the fledgling confidence needed to do it. Forcing a client into structured activity is as unethical as never mentioning it.

- Is the client lonely? I would include 'emotional loneliness', which means they have plenty of contacts, or one special relationship, but they feel distant. Pay particular attention if the client reports being trapped in a relationship.

These issues are only listed here as the most common reasons for ongoing painful emotions, in or out of therapy. No amount of temperature control, new facial expressions, or changed body posture is going to compensate for poor housing, an absence of fulfilling activity or intense loneliness. Keep an eye on the forest as well as the individual trees.

I hope this book has inspired some enthusiasm for teaching emotional regulation, and given an answer to the question, 'But what does that *look* like in individual therapy?' I would be delighted if therapists began to pepper their sessions with the following dialectical phrases:

- On the one hand this, and on the other hand that...
- This much might be too much... this much not enough...
- Sometimes we need to go towards something, sometimes we need to go away from it
- What works for one emotion will not necessarily work for another.

I would also like to think that the steps of emotion regulation have become clearer:

1) Identify the emotion, use the signature features to help
2) Check if the emotion fits the facts in the exact context in which it arose
3) If part of the emotion is valid, work out how to problem-solve whatever it is telling you
4) For the amount of the emotion that is too great, act opposite to the signature features of the emotion

5) If the emotion is too low, or absent, add in the signature features – 'fake it till you make it'.

And finally the most important principle in emotion regulation:

Learn to love your emotions for what they tell you about yourself.

Enjoy the process.

References

Dunkley, C., Borthwick, A., Bartlett, R., Dunkley, L., Palmer, S., Gleeson, S., & Kingdon, D. (2018). Hearing the suicidal patient's emotional pain: A typological model to improve communication. *Crisis: The Journal of Crisis Intervention and Suicide Prevention, 39*(4), 267–274.

Thiruchselvam, R., Blechert, J., Sheppes, G., Rydstrom, A., & Gross, J. J. (2011). The temporal dynamics of emotion regulation: An EEG study of distraction and reappraisal. *Biological psychology, 87*(1), 84–92.

Verduyn, P., Van Mechelen, I., & Tuerlinckx, F. (2011). The relation between event processing and the duration of emotional experience. *Emotion, 11*(1), 20.

Index

For Product Safety Concerns and Information please contact our EU
representative GPSR@taylorandfrancis.com
Taylor & Francis Verlag GmbH, Kaufingerstraße 24, 80331 München, Germany

* 9 7 8 0 3 6 7 2 5 9 2 1 1 *